CHILL PILL

A Stoic Survival Manual for Generation X

BRIAN MURPHY

For
Charlene, Waits, Luken and Otis

TABLE OF CONTENTS

PREFACE

THE GEN X STATE OF THE UNION

Yo. Sup, fellow humans. If you're holding this book expecting a simple self-help redemption story with tidy answers, clean arcs, and a step-by-step plan for a happy ending, get ready for disappointment.

This is a survival manual.

Gen X didn't just grow up in a different time—we grew up in the last stretch of life that was still mostly analog. rotary phones, mixtapes, MTV, pay phones, and the kind of independence that came with a house key on a shoelace and nobody checking in. We learned early that no one was coming to rescue us. Somehow, that became both our burden and our advantage. If you relate to this, you'll get the message in these essays.

Some of these stories aren't "sensitive." But they're not behavioral endorsements, confessions, or instruction manuals either. They're snapshots—memories filtered through the only lens that matters now—distance. Some of what follows is awkward, blunt, or poorly handled—and that's the point. It isn't being defended; it's being illustrated. This is what an unexamined life looks like before perspective develops. If there's a through-line here, it's this: clarity usually arrives late, humility even later, and control over your own reactions is the only human upgrade that actually sticks.

I call it *Pop Stoicism*. Don't worry—it's not a lecture. Stoics weren't trying to be inspirational quote machines. They were trying to survive their own chaos with some dignity intact. Same mission… different soundtrack.

Within these pages you'll see references to classics like Nirvana, Pearl Jam, Soundgarden, *The Breakfast Club*, *Ferris Bueller's Day Off*, *Reality Bites*—not because they were perfect, but because I'm trying to recreate a nostalgic mindset. For just a moment, let's step back to a time when this vibe of music and movies helped a lot of us make sense of life's noise. These movies and songs weren't just entertainment to Gen X; they were the blueprints of our lives. Sometimes good ones. Sometimes flawed ones. But they gave us a way to stand in the mess without completely folding and, in a way, became part of who we are as a generation.

This book moves the way memory moves—in scenes, not steps. Some essays overlap. Some circle the same ideas from different angles. That's intentional. Growth isn't linear, and neither is understanding. The discipline here isn't about becoming calmer, nicer, or more enlightened. It's about staying awake. About learning when to speak, when to shut up, when to push, when to let go, and when to stop mistaking reaction for action.

These stories aren't about Gen X being better than anyone else. They are more like an acknowledgement of how an entire generation became steadier than they used to be because of what they lived through—not despite it. Growing up the way we did wasn't perfect, but it taught us how to improvise, endure, and keep our footing when life gets too loud. Understanding and preserving this process is more valuable now than ever, since some of these abilities are becoming a lost art, even as the world gets busier and chronic anxiety becomes the norm.

If you've ever felt like modern culture moves too fast, the volume never drops, or you're supposed to have everything handled by now—welcome. Breathe in. Take a *Chill Pill*. Embrace your past, and control what you can. Carry the rest with humor and purpose. Even if you were not born between 1965 and 1980, hang in there and enjoy the ride. If you can make it past the *cringe* of Gen X youth, this book may enrich your perspective in ways you never expected.

1

IDOLS

THEY CAN HELP OR HURT KNOW THE DIFFERENCE

"When someone is properly grounded in life, they shouldn't have to look outside themselves for approval."

—Epictetus

The talk was straight to the point.

"Brian, you've got a month to figure it out." *Never going to happen.* "Or I want you to come back down to Los Angeles and work for so-and-so's insurance company. They have jobs there, and you will not have to interview. Buckle down for twenty or thirty years and you can make a decent living as an insurance adjuster in L.A." *I don't think so.*

If you have loving, concerned parents or friends (or you've fucked up enough like I have), there will come a time in your life when you get… the talk. Most people see it coming, even if they can't predict an exact date or time. It's like an intervention about life and employment, and the talk usually includes the damning phrase "working hard or hardly working." For those like me, who felt that life was a pretty sweet ride on an awesome and invincible wave, it can be shocking, annoying as fuck, and downright degrading—especially when that wave is being pushed (funded) by someone else. Get ready. The wipeout is coming, and it is going to drag you across a razor-sharp, shallow reef. Humiliating. Disorienting. It will leave you gasping for air in the dark depths of questioning your very existence.

My "talk" happened on the beautiful island of Coronado. Visiting my parents each summer was heaven. It was usually a week of sand, boogie boarding, pizza, grilling, an assortment of IPAs, and Orange Avenue eye candy which always seemed to rejuvenate my soul. My new career in the entertainment industry was tricky, especially when it came to the idea of financial security. I fell into the category of freelancer, also known as… "you eat what you kill." Sometimes it's hard to kill. Sometimes you don't eat.

So far, there had been a few peaks, many valleys, and even a few gorges in the industry for me. All of my work had been behind-the-scenes production gigs with no imminent upward movement toward higher-paying, steady work. Meanwhile, most of my peers were on their second homes, solid pathways to retirement funds, vacations, money, money, money, blah, blah, blah. None of that mattered to me. I was stoked to have just spent my next month's rent on a custom framed and matted, five-foot-wide Reservoir Dogs cinema poster to hang in my empty Bay Area apartment (special thanks to a dear friend for accepting ownership of the art that now lives in his decked-out BMW/Porsche/Audi service garage).

The 800 lb gorilla in the room was alive, awake, and pacing. My lack of direction. I knew it. I felt it. I ignored it. Church services were over. My dad and I had lunch at the local pizzeria one last time before my flight. My mom stayed back at the condo. Dead giveaway. Dad had crushed his career—solid daily commute to Manhattan, discipline, security, and a financial plan. I never saw him leave for work and, based on his mood or how much I fucked up that day, I rarely wanted to see him at night. Even after a long day of work, train rides home with tired, grumpy, and sometimes drunk businessmen, he still made time to coach our teams. Soccer, baseball, basketball, lacrosse and track—you name it. He was always there for us (and still is). My father was a living example of following "the right path." He worked hard, supported his family, and saved his money to retire with financial security. Of course, now that I have my own family and understand how tough it is to juggle schedules and budgets and homework, I've found another level of respect for my dad. At the time of the talk, though, Dad's example had gone right over my head.

At that time, my dad had just become partner at a global actuarial firm in Los Angeles. His cush retirement plans were imminent. He had sacrificed for this and was not about to let me drain his lifelong dream of golfing every day in the desert. Although I tried my best to stay out of their way financially, I'll admit now that it was never really my priority. Again, finding production work and writing in dimly lit bars in Oakland took precedence over my dad's golf game (thanks, Bukowski).

I had little to say during this conversation, nor was my dad asking for my opinion. The writing was on the wall. *You're going to do what I want you to do. And as a mid-twenties Gen Xer—tough shit. Time to adhere to the Boomer generation.*

Surprisingly, I wasn't too pissed during the talk. By that time of my life, I was very familiar with the "tough-love" routine; however (cue the FOMO violin) I was also very distracted by my thoughts of a massive Halloween party in the Oakland Hills coming up—already rented my costume and everything. Plus, I was stoked about getting back home to continue my passion: attending live music shows, especially one of the greats, Pearl Jam! I had probably already seen Pearl Jam over a dozen times (now it's up to the high forties) and Dad's latest "act-your-age" plans were only slightly penetrating my self-centered state of mind. I thanked my dad for the pizza, and we got into the car. I thought the talk was over. It wasn't. He clearly stated demands, raising his voice to an octave of boiling anger and disappointment. Funny how parents know how to change their voices for maximum impact. Before the end of the car ride, I was so pissed at myself that I almost asked him to stop midway on the Coronado Bay Bridge so I could just jump off and solve the whole problem ASAP. We reached the departure curb at the airport terminal and said good-bye. I exited the car alone and finally understood that this was serious. I was at a crossroad.

I had a late evening nonstop flight up to Oakland, and the airport was empty. I began the long walk toward the gate, passing the rental car counters as I approached the escalator to the departure area. Reeling from the talk, I was struggling to wrap my head around what I was about to endure. Insurance? Sucking up to the man? All my angst and Gen X pride was about to be flushed away. As I trudged miserably down the corridor, noticed a guy at the rental car counter. Actually, I didn't notice him at first, but I noticed his suitcase. I'd seen it before. It was beat up and brown, weathered, and covered in stickers of bands and logos. I couldn't take my eyes off that suitcase. I had seen it so many times on record sleeves, in magazines, in liner notes and Polaroid pictures. I tore my eyes from the case and looked at the customer. Eddie. Fucking. Vedder. Just standing there at the rental car counter.

Two things happened at once: One, I kept walking. As a proud Gen Xer who also worked in film and television, I know how many actors, athletes, and rock stars are bothered everywhere they go. At 11 pm, in an empty corridor, the last thing I wanted to do was antagonize the king of grunge. What would I say anyway? Thankfully, at least a little bit of Stoic philosophy was already running through my veins, cautioning me to avoid chasing fame or wealth, but to measure myself by actions. It probably saved me from a bit more humiliation that day.

Number two: within ten steps of passing my idol, my whole perspective changed. I couldn't help but smile through tears as the transition from "the talk"—to "the walk"–led to a revelation: I wasn't changing shit, and I was not about to be selling insurance. I decided that I would make it work on my own, my way. So, thank you, Eddie Vedder. Thank you for keeping me far away from the nicer things in life like stable jobs, houses with pools, and financial security. Thank you for making it cool to walk around a party, bottle of wine in hand, drinking it all.

Since then, I've remained indebted to this idol, as well as a few others. Staying poor, but true to myself, rather than rich and miserable was the right path for me. "Wanting to be someone else is a waste of the person you are," (Nirvana). When you're twenty, the goal is to be a rock star. When you're forty, the goal is to keep the rock star alive inside a responsible human being. I never abandoned this creed—I evolved it. Integrity plus responsibility. The origin of this idea in my mind now seems ironic, since Vedder is now the lead singer of one of the most influential bands of all time with a net worth of probably hundreds of millions. I wonder what his take on "live the way you want" would be? I may never know, but I'm grateful to him for the inner peace he indirectly gave me.

CALL TO ACTION

When truth cuts deep, do you face it with strength or hide in the comfort of despair? Face it.

2

PARTY LINES, PRANK CALLS, AND PAY PHONES

THE ART OF INTERPERSONAL COMMUNICATION

"First learn the meaning of what you say and then speak."

—Marcus Aurelius

"Hey fuckface… yeah, I'm talking to you, you little piece of shit. Go fuck your mother!"

Click.

"Who is this? You pussy, why don't you meet me at the train station parking lot, and I'll kick your ass."

Click.

"Is this the bowling alley? Do you guys have ten-pound balls? Yeah? How do you walk around then? Bwwaahhh!!"

Click.

Ah… the art of interpersonal communication at its lowest. Before the invention of texting and the current norms of avoiding actual conversations with people, our communication options were limited to pay phones and land lines. The public pay phones were most useful when trying to make prank calls, since you couldn't trace them (this was before the invention of caller ID). It also meant my friends and I were far enough from our parents that they couldn't listen in on the calls. We knew better than to pull this immature, childish crap at home. Out in public, all we needed was a quarter for about two minutes of purely obnoxious, but borderline-creative, behavior for entertainment.

We usually saved the "collect call scam" for when it was absolutely necessary. At times like these, we figured out we were able to call someone "collect" without a quarter by pressing "0" and telling an operator the number we wanted to call. The operator made the call live, without putting us on "hold." We could hear everything.

Once the other person picked up, the operator would say, "Hello, you have a collect call from, caller please state your name [pause for us to speak], would you like to accept the call?" The idea was that the person could either say "yes" and accept the charges of the call, or say "no, fuck off," and hang up. Here's the scam: During the pause intended for our name, while still "live" on the call, we had three-to-five seconds of airtime to relay a free message like,

"Joey—meet me at Scott's five and ten, now!" or "Mom, come pick me up at the field; practice ended early."

Since then, the pay phone and its civil operators have virtually become extinct. What's left is a version of communication where, if someone doesn't recognize your number, they often don't even pick up. And if they do, they usually don't want anything to do with you, since verbal communication is now avoided as often as possible. If you aren't dying, don't bother. 911 is a joke. Right, Flavor Flav?

Another amusing way to kill time back then was calling a party line. For twenty-five cents to a dollar a minute (later charged to the bill of furious parents), a 1-800 number connected us live to anyone else calling in at the same time. No moderator, no rules, pure fun!

When I first discovered this new form of entertainment, I'd jump on the line, run my mouth, act cocky, and pray a girl would hear my stud voice and fall in love. But it was never just me and the sexy girl on the line, and somehow, I always managed to forget that part. It may have sounded like we were alone, but there were always others lurking… listening… waiting. One crack of my voice, one hesitation, and the taunting and ridicule began.

Like many Gen Xers, I was a latchkey kid. This meant I had plenty of time after school every day to get into trouble. One day after school, I was talking to an older woman on the party line. This time, for once, I really felt like I was getting somewhere until, out of left field some guy chimed in to inform me I was a pussy and had no shot. She agreed. Hung up. Silence. Humiliation. I hung up and went back to watching cartoons.

More often, the party lines turned into full-blown verbal chaos. This happened when there were multiple people on the line, all with plenty to say. It was an anarchy of dialogue and verbal chaos with people yelling, posturing, and making plans to meet and fight. Some used it to build reputations:

"Did you hear about me beating the shit out of everyone at the Red Lobster in Hicksville? Oh yeah, go ask around—that was me."

Others used it to schedule the next fight or confrontation. Callers shouted out plans to meet and used the call to describe exactly what they planned to do to each other. I usually stayed quiet during these calls until the *Machos* barked at everyone to get off the line so they could talk, show off, and pray for a girl to come on. This was classic eavesdropping, '80s style… always entertaining!

Folks, humans are losing the art of speaking to one another. No, I don't consider party lines a form of art, but communication is—at least, when it's done in a civilized manner. Now, people avoid talking unless it's necessary. We isolate ourselves and send texts or DMs susceptible to misinterpretations, over analysis, or complete dismissal. Is this really what we want? How does it make us better people?

Emotional intelligence, public speaking, and direct communication will always be necessary for success (sorry, AI). The act of interpersonal communication in the workplace makes us more powerful and prosperous. Skeptical? Go crush a speech in front of a hundred new co-workers. Or better, land a new job because you made eye contact, spoke clearly, and actually connected with someone. These basic communication skills are still applicable and effective today, despite a growing misconception that they are obsolete. Many people today settle for communication channels requiring installation fees, hidden charges, and endless no-tifications instead of a quarter and a little courage. At least there's no more eavesdropping… right, Big Brother?

What my experiences taught me—long before I developed the language to describe it—is that speech is never neutral. The moment we open our mouths, we're making a choice: escalate, retreat, listen, or shut up. Silence can save you, hesitation can sink you, and running your mouth without thinking guarantees consequences. Gen X understands that the fastest way to learn to communicate effectively is to engage with peers with no edit button, no emoji to soften intent, and no delete. We spoke, or we didn't—and we owned the results. This practice prepared us for the world of adult consequences.

CALL TO ACTION

The fool reacts. Choose to speak (or text) with intention and restraint—and only after thoughtful reflection.

3

THE LATCHKEY LIFESTYLE

SCRAMBLED SOFT PORN, INGENUITY, CARTOON VIOLENCE, AND ANARCHY

"Happiness is a good flow of life."

—Zeno of Citium

One day after school, my friend convinced me that there was a treasure trove of "nudie" mags in the sewer dump by our house. After cutting a hole in the barbed wire fence, we dropped into at least three feet of mud (more likely shit) and poked around. I don't know how he knew they would be there, but he was correct. It was like we'd found Davy Jones' locker but covered in shit. This is no exaggeration. I literally mean actual, terrible, putrid, sewer shit. The smell is forever burned into my memory. As I pulled one of the mags from the noxious sludge and carefully separated the clammy, oozing pages, I found myself gawking at a large, clean-shaven… penis. *What. The. Fuck.* I almost vomited. I peeled another page over. Same. I looked up at my friend for answers, but he had the same look. We had gone through all that nastiness for gay magazines… not that there's anything wrong with that (right, Seinfeld?), but gay porn wasn't exactly what we were after. Our defeated, stinking asses climbed back up the hill and out of the sewer dump. The memory of that stench is still sometimes triggered when I visit certain dive bars or subway stations, and I laugh every time… not that there's anything wrong with that.

As a side note for anyone who has never watched Seinfeld, on an episode called "The Outing," one of the writers received a pre-airing concern that the subject of homosexuality as it was referenced may be too controversial for television. During the discussion, a comment was made by one of the writers ending in the phrase, "… not that there's anything wrong with that." Seinfeld thought it was so funny, he used the line in that episode not once, but eight times.

You may be wondering where my parents were while I was sewer diving for porn mags. I was a latchkey kid, remember? If you are from my generation, you know exactly what that means and were probably out having your own unsupervised adventures at my age. But for any readers not familiar with the term, here's my experience: For a long period in my life (K-8th grade), I walked to and from school every day alone. Like so many other latchkey kids, I kept my house key on a necklace under my school uniform. The necklace was not a cool silver chain from Spencer's that may have been admired by females—no. For most of us, it was an old shoelace or a piece of yarn threaded through a house key and tied into a "necklace." Not sexy. Sometimes I just kept it in my pocket, which was risky since I knew that if I lost it, I'd be sitting out on the stoop in front of my house for a good two hours until Mom got home. Rain or shine. Hot or cold. After that, I got to Mom's screaming about my stupidity. It happened. It was part of the Gen X law of tough shit.

Sulking over a lost key is like watching a poorly edited movie—replaying it never changes the ending. Stoics understand that the only stage of life we have control over is the one we're in right now, so keep your eyes forward and don't unpack regrets like souvenirs. What's done is done. Get over it and move on. The law of tough shit!

Once I was home, usually with around two hours to kill, I watched cartoons. After that, the family usually watched the news or a Mets game while we ate "TV dinners" (frozen microwavable meals). Both were usually very disappointing. This was how technology looked when I was a kid. It was before flat screens and digital TV modules, and we had what was called "the box." It was the size of a Kleenex box with buttons numbered one through thirteen. A short cord attached the box to the television. If you were rich enough, you could buy an extension for this cord, which allowed you to sit back on your couch or recliner to change channels. Back in middle school, rumors started to swirl that some wizard (who must be running NASA by now) figured out that if you pressed the numbers 3 and 5 at the same time, your screen would scramble and cut to the Playboy channel. This channel was the closest thing Gen X had to porn besides Cinemax (aka "Skin"emax), HBO (late night), and physical magazines that you either tried to read in a store (never worked), tried to peek at while you waited for a haircut (never worked), pulled from the sewer mud (you read how that turned out) or stolen from mailboxes on your paper route (always worked—I'll explain later). Once you pressed the magic numbers, a highly scrambled screen appeared allowing a few glorious seconds to view the "good stuff." True, there was no actual sex, but there were lots of half-dressed girls whispering risqué proverbs at the screen. Sometimes I would get a full two seconds of boob, maybe an ass, or if lucky, the sight of an unshaven vagina. Don't judge, I was young. There was no sex-ed in my parochial school, and I did not even know what I was watching, but it felt great. When the two seconds were done, I had to outwit the box again. Usually, I got only two or three successful glimpses of sexy images; after that, it was back to regular TV with a boner.

Other than scraps of forbidden porn, there were several television programs I watched religiously as a kid. Believe it or not, a few offered surprisingly deep insight into life, and some of these shows molded my psyche.

The Little Rascals (Our Gang)

These guys were great. A live-action, mostly black-and-white series created from the *Our Gang* shorts of the 1920s. The series first appeared on television in the mid-50s, and I watched reruns every afternoon throughout my childhood. *The Little Rascals* had the best comedic lineup and a consistently entertaining, diverse crew of characters. The characters shifted a bit each season, but Spanky, Alfalfa, Buckwheat, Darla, and Petey the dog were staples. The show featured incredibly attractive teachers, stereotypically Irish tough cops, and superb comedic performances from the storekeepers, dog catchers, and the jealous husbands of the attractive teachers. Like I said, the gang was diverse, yet they got along perfectly. Sure, there was fighting and arguments, but they were all for the same cause. Usually, the best idea or answer became the goal, and if it didn't succeed, they learned a lesson for next time.

The Little Rascals taught me that the most diverse teams are usually the best teams. It showed me that when solving problems, it's best to leave our egos at the door, accept and welcome constructive criticism, ask thought-provoking questions, and then figure out a coherent linear strategy that everyone can believe in. The best idea will win… just don't drink the milk (if you know, you know). I have applied these Little Rascal lessons to my own life with great results.

Tom & Jerry (original version)

Tom (the cat) and Jerry (the mouse) were comedic, violent, and had a strange love/hate relationship. In each episode, they took turns trying, and almost always succeeding, to annoy the shit out of each other. It's like they had nothing better to do each day, or maybe it was a religious calling. Who knows? But it worked for them. Like savvy engineers and petty criminals, they plotted out each mission to maim the other. Some plans were quite horrifying, some were hilarious, but you always knew that at the end of the day (or episode), they would become best friends. Accepting their differences, they expected nothing more from their waxing and waning feuds.

Sometimes I wish the world would take a deep breath and study Tom and Jerry to parlay what they learn into current society. There's way too much friction between people these days. Society seems to embrace the attitude of "if you don't give back just as hard to the next person, you are soft." Why not try to understand that we are all just "Toms" and "Jerrys," and at the end of the day, instead of focusing only on our differences, we should remember that we are all just people trying to survive? If you see someone you hate hanging from a cliff, why not pull them to safety instead of pushing them down? Afterward, you can decide to hit them over the head with a cast iron skillet (kidding, of course). The point is, when you engage with friends, (or enemies) be fearless, but not reckless. Hold on to your humanity and keep to your morals. It's okay to agree to disagree.

The Young Ones

This was a Sunday night British sitcom which used to air on a once-very-cool music television channel. Watching this was a perfect way to end a crazy weekend and diminished traces of the "scary Sundays." (For the record, I never understood that term until I got older, and I never subscribed to its worthless mantra. Why can't Monday be the best day of the week? To hell with that.)

Anyway, this show had it all… four flat mates sharing a rundown apartment in the UK: Rik, Vyvyan, Mike, and Neil. These guys couldn't have been more different from each other in terms of political views, musical taste, bathing habits, or socioeconomic scale. This was a great set up for either tragedy or hilarity. Somehow, they all managed to survive each week without killing each other. The characters were relatable because they dealt with the same Gen X dilemma we did—we were all expected to accept whatever life handed us and allow the powers in charge (boomers) to handle our futures (only to see shit blow up later in our faces).

The Young Ones also taught us the value of not selling out. They produced only 12 episodes for one season. The run length had already decided this before the first show aired, and despite the show's positive reception, the creators didn't alter the plan. They stood their ground and made the most out of every episode, each ending with some sort of tantalizing message. The messages were sometimes extremely violent yet still had you laughing through the closing credits as you brushed your teeth and got amped for Monday morning. You know what else I learned from the show? Friendships are important, but quality is much more important than quantity.

CALL TO ACTION

Adversity doesn't count your friends—it reveals them. As you grow, choose friends who stick around, even when it costs them.

4

PROBLEM SOLVING

BEFORE THE STREET LIGHTS TURNED ON

"The important thing about a problem is not its solution, but the strength we gain in finding the solution."

—Seneca

During summers, parents of Gen Xers drank beer and smoked while driving us around in the front seat, no seat belts, and the car windows rolled up. Playgrounds were metal and we were lucky if they weren't rusted. There was not much support if we fell, no padding to calm nerves or protect bones… it was concrete on top of concrete. We learned to fall cautiously and understood that no one was coming to help us.

This general environment of childhood danger sets the stage for occasional days when certain groups of friends went into "engineer mode," using junk found around the neighborhood. Once, my neighborhood group built a ramp out of a stolen milk crates and a somewhat-stable wooden board. Someone always had to go first to test the invention. I wish there was a simple word to describe the feelings surrounding that first jump to later generations. It would have to encompass a youthfully passionate mix of pride, excitement, adrenaline, and fear. Sure, I sometimes launched straight over the handlebars, or worse, landed on my back with the wind knocked out of me, but I felt a such a sense of accomplishment and pride as I gasped to regain a normal breathing pattern. Nine times out of ten, my friends were already pissing their pants laughing and enjoying my misery. True, what started off exciting occasionally ended with severe injuries. However, as the sun slowly sank behind our houses, this sense of measured danger is what made Gen X kids feel alive. Finding, or in this case building, an element of value into an otherwise slow-moving day is a skill we should all master. There is just something exhilarating about knowing that another adventure can be waiting for us the very next day.

The neighborhood streetlights served as a checkered flag: time to collect your thoughts, your emotions, and leave it all behind. Most communities I lived in didn't give two shits about damaged stop signs or potholes. On Long Island, however, the parents saw to it that whoever kept the streetlights on at dusk was paid promptly. Our tax dollars gave us street discipline and accountability. It was black or white. You either made it home as soon as those lights went on, or you were toast.

"Oh, didn't you see the lights come on? Well then, where the fuck were you?" You'd better have a suitable answer to that one (hint: there were no suitable answers).

Seneca, the Roman philosopher, nailed it when he said, "Train your mind to welcome adversity, and do not fear it." I agree completely…. game freakin' on! Society often forgets how blessed we are to endure at least one adventure per day in our lives. Some folks have more, but everyone can have at least one in a day. The happiest people know how to recognize or create these each day, appreciating both peaks and valleys of the concept. Looking back and acknowledging the day's adventure, whether or not the outcome was what we expected, can make us feel alive no matter our ages.

I miss my childhood adventures. Since most of them ended in some pretty important (and sometimes painful) life lessons, it should be no surprise that they usually began in the form of a question. Some were positive, like how I was going to get the high score on Galaga with only two quarters, or how I could get the local new-wave girl to notice me. Others, I'll admit, were sort of seedy like what's the best way to peep quietly through a neighbor's fence to observe a hot MILF sunning herself in a skimpy leopard bikini by her pool. More than once, I began the day hiding under my bedroom window to peer outside as the three college-aged sisters across the street laid-out in the sun to tan with practically nothing on. Wowzah! Some adventures were dangerous, like how to get home from playing wall ball against a local brick building without the town bullies harassing me or getting bitten by the crazy neighbor's dog. Looking back now, I realize my childhood wasn't just cartoons and chaos—it was also about perspective. "Screws fall out all the time, the world's an imperfect place," (The Breakfast Club). That line hits differently when you've actually lived through a few adventures.

You know what all these adventures had in common? An opportunity to adapt. Gen X knows the importance of adaptation. We accept it as a daily certainty. It was imperative to our survival. Sitting curbside for hours, we figured out how to properly ollie on a shitty concrete street. Repetition. Never quitting. The bloody knees and sometimes lips or noses strengthened us. After all, the last thing we wanted to do was go home and complain to our parents. They had no desire to deal with our childish problems and rarely listened anyway. It's just the way things were. The answers we needed about life weren't handed to us as the streetlights came on and the crappy TVs said, "good evening." We figured these answers out for ourselves by making mistakes and learning from them, and it made us independent. The streetlights may be LED now, but they still come on at dusk, and so does my gratitude for another day's adventure.

Problem solving before the streetlights came on taught me not to let problems linger, but to figure them out before the end of the day. Sounds simple, right? Maybe, but most of life's problems are just tiny instances of life—merely minuscule specks—in the grand scheme of things. Skeptical? Consider the "overview effect," described by astronauts on the International Space Station. It is a cognitive shift characterized as a state of awe and a sense of interconnectedness often experienced by astronauts while gazing through the windows of the spacecraft. Sometimes they notice it while completing an exterior task in space, often reporting an overwhelming sense of the planet's fragility and the importance of cooperation and unity among humans. What does this teach us? Maybe we should stop complaining and take care of ourselves and others. Is one life more important than another? How important are the activities that take up most of your time each day? How many likes or DMs do you require to release those precious, addictive endorphins? Is it worth your investment in the grand scheme? If not, stop it. Simple.

CALL TO ACTION

Every stumble teaches us where control ends and clarity of purpose begins. Don't be afraid to make mistakes.

5

MIXTAPES SPEAK LOUDER THAN TEXTS

"If you accomplish something good with hard work, the labor passes quickly, but the good endures; if you do something shameful in pursuit of pleasure, the pleasure passes quickly, but the shame endures."

—Gaius Musonius Rufus

Listen up! Pull your eyes away from the screen for a second. What if you could send only one text a day? One message. One person. No edits. No mulligans. And you had to include a photo that encapsulates your day. Who would you send it to? Why? What would it say? What image would you send? Welcome to the world of mixtapes: audio cassettes for the avant-garde. Gen X remembers them well—plastic rectangles with spools of film inside like spaghetti strips. My heart goes out to any readers still unfamiliar with this icon of the '70s and '80s music scene. Most of these audio jewels came in a one-hour format (30 minutes of recordable tape per side), but if you really cared about someone, you went bigger. Two hours of blank cassette tape meant commitment.

The tricky part was deciding what to record and how. Compared to the last decade, Gen X grew up practically starved in terms of music technology. We did not have music available to us "on demand." There was no skipping, no editing. If you were broke, you had to record music straight from the radio. To make a mixtape, this required hitting the *record* and *play* buttons on a rickety radio player (aka "boom box") at exactly the right time. Huge decisions went into this ahead of time, especially if you didn't want the DJ banter in the recording before the song. The anxiety from anticipating the exact moment to press *record* was harrowing. To make the situation more stressful, there was no way to tell what the radio DJ would even play. That meant we sometimes had to wait hours for a particular song. Split-second reaction time was imperative. Assuming the recording went well, we still had to hit the *stop* (or *pause*) button before the next song began or a commercial came on. Songs with long fadeouts made it much easier, but if it was a quick, climatic ending, fast reflexes were key. Miss it?

Too bad. Start over. And God help you if the DJ talked over the intro or the station became staticky during the recording. Don't forget, radio was not digital for a very long time, so your antenna-reception mojo had to be tight for this to work.

The invention of CDs changed the game. If you managed to save enough to buy a radio with a CD player, the possibilities were endless. When I finally got mine, I sat at my kitchen table for hours thinking about that special person and planning the perfect playlist. Production of a mixtape took patience, effort, and thought. That's what made it matter! It showed people you thought about them long enough to create something that took a long time, very intentional planning, and a lot of work. Today, we can send a heart emoji in half a second. Back then, it might have taken three days to convey the same message. Because of this, we learned to embrace the philosophy of "right time, right moment," and we made it work.

A good mixtape also revealed something about the creator: strengths, weaknesses, musical knowledge, and even some insight into character. Side A got the listener's attention. It typically featured the best songs and the greatest attention to detail. But side B revealed the true commitment level and proved who we really were. It was an obvious display of either perseverance and musical skill or an embarrassing lack of creativity. Often, our initial intentions for the tape morphed into something else by the end of side B. In any case, a good mixtape usually left a person exhausted both mentally and physically. Gen X learned a lot about ourselves making mixtapes.

Once the music is recorded, we had to decide on artwork and liner notes. With only a space the size of an index card to work with, we had to write each song on the inside sleeve of the case. If you cared a lot about the recipient, the tiniest details of the process could become overwhelming. Should I leave it blank and just color it? Maybe draw something onto the tape itself? Fat markers or thin Sharpie pens? Give me a break. I'm getting anxiety just thinking about it!

Does Gen Z even feel anxiety when they snap, text, or post? How could they when it happens all day every day? I worry about the general conformity to this modern standard of less-than-mindful communication. If we've reached a point where we can no longer lie in bed at night and remember every text, snap, post, or like we communicated that day, then it is no longer meaningful communication. It's just noise. Quantity over quality. It's waste.

This isn't about attacking modern communication. It's about awareness. Strengths and weaknesses exist in every generation, and they often reveal the direction we are headed as a country, a culture, a civilization, or a united world. In this case, if we ignore our weakness of communication, we could lose the ability to mean what we say and to be understood. By making it a habit to acknowledge what makes us weak both mentally and physically, we can find our centers and stay sane in a chaotic world. In doing so, our weaknesses become strengths.

Obviously, mixtapes are a passionate subject for me. I haven't even told you the most challenging part: the long wait for approval after giving the tape away. It shouldn't matter, but it always does, and it is painful when that approval never comes. I always tried not to care. I only made it to be thoughtful, not to earn praise. But rejection always sucks, and it hits even harder when a lot of time and effort was put into the gift. Most Gen X teens had to spend a lot of time building ourselves back up after rejection, and we turned out fine. Gritty, even. We learned to move on. Make another one. Keep going. Sometimes the lesson is in the process, not the result.

We will all be better off if we can remember the flow of the journey we want to be on. As we journey, life will send us onto peaks and into valleys. My advice: take a deep breath, remind yourself of the big picture of your overall path, and all will be well. Be aware that your greatest strength might also be a weakness? Test this idea by asking yourself, "Is this strength not only helping me but also inspiring someone else? Is my strength providing value to a relationship or a job or a societal need?" Examine your weaknesses the same way. Life is full of opportunities to improve, so use them: long walks, meditation and an honest understanding of your values and levels of consciousness.

Throughout life, I've given away many mixtapes. Most recipients graciously accepted them. I still remember every single one. I hope it brightened their days. Every year at Christmas, my middle school classmates and I were forced to bring a Kris Kringle gift for someone in the class. Although blind luck determined which gift you received, when someone saw a present from me, they geeked out. After tearing the wrapping paper off, they became the proud owner of an original "Murph mixtape." No matter what was on it, I'm proud to admit they all considered the tapes worthy of bragging rights when they got to be a part of the Murph mixtape club. Along with an intoxicating hit of approval, I knew that my patience and diligence paid off.

My point, I guess, is this: the mixtape symbolizes giving in its purest sense. It is the gift of time, of effort, of thought, and of self. Life should be the same. It's OK to edit life and figure out how to proceed. But remind yourself occasionally that less can be more, and sometimes the lesson truly lies in the journey, not the outcome.

So many stories and reasons fill the "why's" of life, and I truly believe in some kind of cosmic correlation between our reasoning and a project like this. Keep life exciting by treating it like a mixtape. Hit the record and play buttons and live intentionally and for others. There is no need to validate yourself to the world by constantly emitting the same message repeatedly like a lame radio station. Keep it fresh. Use what you have to work with wisely and cut the parts that don't fit your purpose. I sometimes think that if I won the lottery, I would vanish from society and live on a plot of land with so many acres no one could see me. Do I really need to win the lottery for that? Probably not. Plan your mixtape of life according to your purpose and give it as a gift to your spiritual growth. Just be sure to adjust the antenna and smooth out the static first.

CALL TO ACTION

Take the advice of Axl Rose and practice patience each day…
just a little patience.

6

ROTATING BACKDROPS

ONE STAGE

"The universe is change; our life is what our thoughts make it."

—Marcus Aurelius

Ahh, change… the story of life. My immediate advice? Live as many places as possible before settling down. Exploring new places will not only scare the hell out of you but also give you the mental "know-how" to think clearly and with a unique, diverse perspective as you move out of adolescence and into full-blown adulthood.

I've always wanted to live in different places. People thought I was nuts for moving from Long Island to California for college.

But even though I didn't know anything about the Golden State, it set the tone of my life for many years. When people ask me where I'm from, I have to stop and think… you mean right now? Ten years ago? Mentally? Originally? When I was younger, my mixtape DJ name was "WYCF," shorthand for "Where Y'all Coming From?"—a pretty important question to ask yourself from time to time. I'm not ashamed to admit I come from a hybrid of places. Some even consider me a "mutt." Don't feel bad for me—I don't. A life of wandering is full of mystery and excitement. Who knows what's coming over the horizon? I learned to take it all in as an experiment. If doing the same thing every day is your cup of tea, that's fine. Just don't be surprised if it starts to feel heavy. Life is a book with many chapters, and it's up to us to figure out when a chapter should end and another should begin. What will your story be about? It's worth some thought. Turn your focus within, breathe in and breathe out, and find that inner peace. You can search that quiet space within you to find the plot of your story and guide your remaining chapters. Here are a few anecdotes from the chapters of my life, but my "book" isn't even close to being complete.

Strong Island

Although I was born in Brooklyn, I don't have clear memories of it. We moved to Long "Strong" Island, (Nassau County, Syosset to be specific) in the 70s and I began to realize how nuts New York could be. Living in the shadow of the city meant seeing it all—burnt-out cars, abandoned buildings, desolate streets. Scary stuff. Going back to Brooklyn or NYC to visit relatives felt like preparing for battle. We never really knew what to expect, whether we would encounter allies or enemies on the journey, or even if we would arrive safely, but we knew to be ready for anything. The drive was a white-knuckle experience, but we only took the LIRR (Long Island Railroad) when we had no other choice, since the train felt even less safe than driving. Either way, we always felt safe once we arrived… at least until it was time to leave. After that, the anxiety returned until we reached the Long Island Expressway and headed back to the suburbs.

The people of Long Island wore unofficial badges of honor based on the area of the island they called home. In my mind, I just broke it down to Nassau or Suffolk counties. As a kid, I noticed people categorized each other by asking how close they lived to NYC or how long it took them to get there by train. I lived pretty close. As a teen, I was adventurous enough to escape the suburbs often via the LIRR to wind up in heaven… a.k.a., Penn Station. I loved hanging out there. The sights and smells were amazing except the bathrooms, which were probably among the nastiest in the world. Penn Station was a great place to hit up the underground markets and peruse the giant glass coolers filled with Budweiser tall boys, especially since they'd sell to anyone with money. Brilliant!

Heading back to Long Island after a city adventure was like heading back to reality from Fantasyland. Long Island folks worked their tails off. Everybody there busted ass to make ends meet for their families. The culture of the area was intense, and sometimes even comically violent. Each summer, we'd swim at the community pool after my parents got off work. On weeknights, an adult softball league played on an adjacent field while we swam. After multiple cannonballs and can openers, I sometimes crossed the parking lot to check out the "game." I was not there to watch them actually play, however. I was there for the fights. I scouted the teams early each season to find out which ones were there strictly for the game, and which participated for different reasons. I was there for the latter. At one game, there was a team made up of hometown faces and represented by the local sports pub playing another team who was not local. They dressed in black, rode motorcycles to games, and had uniforms that looked like a cross between the Pittsburgh Pirates and the Oakland Raiders. It was funny as hell, but I dared not crack a smile in front of them. I figured out which night they would fight each other (I mean, "play") and made sure I had the best seat in the stands. The tension began with the first pitch.

Of course, both teams were competitive and wanted to win the game, but more importantly, they also wanted to be the alpha. I'll never forget the moment in mid-game, when the shit-talking from both benches was at its peak, and someone shouted, "We can't fight with the kid in the stands." I looked around and realized they were talking about me. I waited until the inning was over and made sure everyone saw me leave. They probably thought I was going back to the swimming pool. Instead, I hid between two cars in the parking lot and watched in secret. Sure as shit, the very next inning, on a routine double-play, I saw the runner slide cleats up and (pretty much) fists up. Benches cleared, and it was on! Maybe it was the stress of a hard day's work, or just being on Long Island, but these brawls would have put MLB (or even the Latin American League) fights to shame. Once the fuse went off… the game was over. Extra innings (a.k.a., side fights) continued at the sports pub later that evening. I had homework to do and could not attend.

The "Yay"

Landing at SFO for college taught me very quickly that California (specifically the San Francisco Bay Area—aka "The Yay") was not what I expected it to be. As a New York native, I thought that all of California was palm trees, sand, and bikinis. Naïve? Absolutely. Turns out, I didn't know shit. This dose of reality was my first adult opportunity to adapt and learn away from home.

Lesson one: bad (or no) communication will always end poorly. This thought had plenty of time to sink in as I waited for my ride to pick me up from the airport… for two hours. The "college representative" did seem to consider me a top priority. Tapping into skills from my latchkey days, I made the best of the time. At baggage claim, I noticed that if I collected the luggage dollies that were rented and abandoned, and then pushed them back into their mechanical corrals, the machine would spit out $.75 per dolly. I made about ten bucks while I waited! It was awesome until Murphy's law reared its ugly head, and I had to spend my newfound cash on several packs of underwear. I completely forgot to pack any. I was an immature eighteen-year-old about to start a month-long training camp for soccer and didn't bring a single pair of underwear. Lesson two: don't forget to pack underwear.

Time passed, and I settled into the experience of living in the Yay. The rhythm of my life revolved around raves, illicit dance parties, and clubs. I could get in just about anywhere with my fake ID, and these parties were off the chart! Knowing which telephone pole or storefront would reveal the latest DIY flyer cryptically disclosing the whereabouts of these events was next-level Indiana Jones mentality. Warehouses in super seedy locations would suddenly flood with people appearing out of nowhere. No lines or guest lists… just people from all walks of life. Inside was an experience of pure joy. Everyone felt it… the excitement, the mystery, the anticipation of, "Holy shit… this is pretty cool and may turn into something." As an adult who continues to spin vinyl, I'm glad house and techno are still around. Third lesson: dig deep into your favorite music genre and find the pioneers. Listen to the best and don't settle.

Another lesson from the Yay: People's Park in Berkeley back in the 80s and 90s was exactly what the stereotype suggests—a dangerous, chaotic, counterculture haven. When I first roamed "Bezerkeley," it was comprised of multiple record stores, pizzerias, bookstores, and microbrew taverns. I loved every square inch of it. Parking was easy because the area was not safe, so my NY street smarts came in handy. Stepping out of the vehicle along the edges of the park involved sidestepping a cornucopia of homeless people, addicts, and gang bangers staring you down. So, when locking my car and heading toward the fun, I gave them a simple nod while telepathically begging, "Please—don't fuck with my car?" No one ever bothered my car, but I still managed to get into some trouble in the area.

Lesson four: don't piss in public. This was a tough lesson for me, since the court-order that resulted demanded many hours of community service in that same area. I spent a week serving breakfast to the homeless of People's Park. After partying in that area so many times, this new role felt very surreal. I had to be at the church kitchen at 4 a.m. each day to make the food (oatmeal and toast), count the hard-boiled eggs, and load up my car to serve by 6 a.m. One morning, as I hustled into the church, another guy was walking out to smoke a cigarette. Dressed in full clerical garb, I was astonished to realize it was the dean of discipline from my college. I was surprised, since he had never mentioned being a church pastor during our "discussions" in his office. This Reverend had to deal with a lot of my college immaturity (yes, shame on me, I know), but we always hit it off. We had a routine: I got into trouble, he let me have it, and then we sat around to shoot the shit for a minute or two. It was nothing personal. That brings me to lesson five: When you do something stupid, just own it. Don't lie. The punishment is over more quickly that way and you can move on to shooting the shit. Anyway, when he saw me loading up my car, he gave me a nod of approval. Respect. It was a first, and it felt good.

My California experience is incomplete without mentioning Tilden Park. Located in the hills of Berkeley, Tilden Park has the best views of the Golden Gate Bridge to one side and Mount Diablo in the East Bay. In my mid-twenties, I ran my ass off on those trails training for marathons. To this day, if I'm visiting the area and need a minute to breathe, that's where I go. The park is like the *Mutual of Omaha's Wild Kingdom!* While visiting, I've had a bobcat stalk me, I've jumped over too many rattlesnakes to count, and I've been scared shitless by other runners appearing unexpectedly out of the fog. Running in that park changed my life, and I still consider it one of the best places in the country to mentally regroup and contemplate life.

Hell A

Lesson six: For any bright-eyed folks who want to live the "Hollywood dream," consider setting boundaries first:

a timeline, accountability checkpoints, daily goals, etc. You should also consider finding a mentor that will not sugarcoat shit. The truth hurts, especially in Tinsel Town, but it can save you from wasting a huge chunk of your life. The truth is, LA has a way of wrapping itself around you like a warm blanket. Way too comfortable. Before you realize it, five years has passed and you've made no progress towards your original dream. Working freelance in the "industry" can take you to the four corners of the world and/or the Valley. But, if you never had any desire to end up in the Valley (or wherever Hell A spit you out), it's best to set some clear boundaries before the ride begins. Back in the day, live television projects made up a large percentage of available Hollywood jobs. These jobs were always high energy, and when you had the right production team in place, it was such a rush on filming days. Working at the Academy Awards was a good example of this. As a novice screenwriter, it was a trip to see Matt Damon and Ben Affleck backstage before they won the award for best screenplay. Watching their lives change forever in real time… inspirational.

Back then, huge amounts of money and corporate airtime went into the production of network television award shows. Sometimes those budgets allowed employees to work internationally. One of my travel gigs was in Monte Carlo. For over a month, I got to call Monaco my home. Holy moly! While there, I received an invitation to lunch on a yacht moored just outside the luxurious harbor. Soon after arriving, my street-smart alarm went off as I noticed a half dozen suit-wearing, machine-gun-wielding gents guarding the boat. I nervously stepped onto the dinghy to transfer from the shore to the yacht (hell yes, I still boarded!) wondering why the security was so extreme. *All this gun play just for some lunch?* As soon as I boarded, I understood. We were greeted by Nelson Mandela! He was waiting to shake hands with the dozen guests who were joining him from the production. For a moment, I was terrified—I mean like, shit-my-pants terrified—but not for long. The arrogance of my youth has saved me from all sorts of reasonable reactions, both before that moment and since then, and it didn't let me down on that yacht. I am embarrassed now to admit that I didn't value the time I spent with this world-renowned figure. As The Great Nelson Mandela sat at the far end of the table and discussed the peace efforts he was envisioning for the world and the wisdom he gained during his reflection in prison, I was actually a bit annoyed. (Again, I am not proud of this, but my current reflection demands honesty). My focus at the time was back on shore, thinking about the upcoming night.

Somehow, I had made it onto the list for a Victoria's Secret private party at Jimmy's nightclub and Boy George was set to DJ! I couldn't have cared less about the words and wisdom of Nelson Mandela. *Shame on you, Murph!*

Years later, the wear and tear of the fast-paced freelance lifestyle caught up to me. I was done. Oddly enough, I feel like my career in Los Angeles ended by running full circle back to the idea of family. At the time, I worked with a very close-knit group. To me, they were family. With all sincerity, Adam Sandler is the most legit guy around. The GOAT of class acts. He is a family guy who stays loyal to his friends. Genuine would be an understatement when describing his character. I treasured his spirit and goodwill and feel like most of Hollywood could learn a thing or two from the Sandman. The spirit of family I felt working in his office, however, filled me with a need to better care for my own new family. This required a parting of ways, but I will forever treasure my Hollywood family.

The Big Easy

If you give love to NOLA, she will give it right back to you. My experiences in New Orleans were extremely diverse. Weeks with no power on the North Shore after Katrina while enjoying fresh grilled fish and all the other food from the useless, melting garage freezers was an opportunity to adapt I hope to never experience again. Multiple stints in the dive bars of Orleans Parish taught me the meaning of a true regular. I served as a tour guide for friends through the Bywater and Marigny (special ones), Uptown and Garden District (more refined ones), Vieux Carre, and Bourbon Street (all of them) and learned to respect everything about New Orleans. For visitors to the area—show your heart to NOLA, and she will return it with a big ole' hug and watch over you. For the locals—relentless focus, refuse drama.

The Sip

Where do I even start with this? Holy shit. I mean, I'm writing this book from the Mississippi Gulf Coast where I've lived for over a decade. William Faulkner once penned, "To understand the world, you have to understand a place like Mississippi," I might go to my grave contemplating what he meant. Grace. Service above self. Attitude of gratitude. These are themes that crept into my life almost immediately after moving to the Deep South. I know, I know… how the fuck could you move down there after living in such big, vibrant cities? And, once again, my reply is… rotating backdrops, one stage. Many chapters, one book. And of course, I now have to add in the old cliché that once you become a parent, you do whatever it takes to elevate your kids and give them the best chances of success. Mississippi still offers the best chance for my kids to be happy and successful in the world. Here's how it all went down:

Act One: The Drive

I sent my family down on a plane to keep their spirits up and their asses out of the situation I was about to endure. Mississippi wasn't new to us. We'd been visiting the Gulf Coast for over twenty years and often talked about retiring on the "third coast." However, uprooting a wife and two young boys, without first having jobs or job-leads, was a gamble even for me. Mind you, we did have family down here. During our transition, they provided us with a home-cooked meal or two and an involuntary Bible study, but that was about it. There was also a kind man from my in-laws' church who got wind of us coming and donated a $20 bill to help us out. I later learned the guy really didn't have $20 to give, so we were especially touched by his generosity. More importantly, we were comforted by his willingness to teach us what people mean when they talk about Southern hospitality. It's why we love the Sip so much.

The stress and exhaustion from driving a U-Haul across the country over three days had started to make me feel numb. As I came around the last bend to our new home, I can't tell you how relieved I felt to see smiling family members waiting to help unload the truck, put dishes and clothes away, mount the TV screen, and build the kids' beds. With all those people helping, I don't think it took more than an hour to make the house functional. As I absorbed the unselfish gestures of my new community, I arranged for a case of ice-cold beer to be at the ready for all the helpers, although none of them drank. Oh well, I guess my first day in Mississippi was destined to involve some "Bud Heavies." My first night was sleepless thanks to the nonstop soundtrack of the most violent thunderstorm I had ever heard. A sign? Lesson learned: Keep beer around for storms.

Act Two: Employment

When you're unemployed in a new state with no connections, the right thing to do is to provide for your family by any means necessary. In other words, you take any damn job that is available—at least for the time being. You want to see what a real man is? Look for the one that understands the assignment—provide for the family. No questions. No excuses. Non-negotiable. Just fucking get at it. Poverty is undesirable no matter where you live, but especially in Mississippi. When an area has fewer resources in general, it also has fewer resources for people in need. Since my needy boat was not leaving the harbor soon, I started looking for a job right away.

My first Mississippi employment wasn't exactly a graveyard shift, but it wasn't a nine to five either. The job was at a packaging center in the middle of nowhere with a clock-in at 3am. Sometimes the trucks were already there when I arrived, sometimes we had to wait a while, but when it got there, me and about twenty other grunts had to unload them, throw the packages down cavernous conveyor belt ramps, and then sort them into piles based on tiny labels. The packages were then reloaded onto trucks by the drivers. I wore all black. Black boots. Black gloves. And I kept a gallon jug of water next to me. I'm pretty sure I looked like a psycho, but I fucking crushed that job, especially compared to the lifers. I could always tell they were lifers from the quality of their work (or lack thereof). I sweated and busted my ass for that paycheck and was grateful. Makin' due, getting by.

The next job I landed had me reconsidering a corporate route (cheers, Dad!). I found a job on the campus of the John C. Stennis Space Center. This place was huge and outstanding. JFK once stated that any rocket going into space must get there through Hancock County, and I understood why. The campus was sprawling and prevalent. A variety of agencies and veteran-run companies were housed within the campus walls. Most of these buildings were just gigantic rooms with cubicles and plenty of pictures of space shuttles in various forms of production and execution. My shift was rough. I arrived at 7pm and didn't clock out until 6am. There was only one other guy or gal with me in the entire bullpen. Our job was to take calls through the night to help folks troubleshoot computer tech issues. I sometimes struggled with what to say. There often seemed to be a feeling of terrible loneliness on both ends of the phone. Maybe it was because I was speaking to people from around the world, I'm not sure, but I began to sense a sort of camaraderie with the people who called that got me through my shift. The shifts often ended with an early morning roll into the commissary where most early risers were grabbing coffee and donuts, and then rolling back out with a tallboy sixer. Eventually, the overnight cycle started to wear me down. Luckily, I found a much more relaxed, though lower paying, job working as a farmhand at a local horse ranch. The farm owner trained horses and offered riding lessons to kids. I didn't have set hours. Just projects.

She just told me once to clear a fence that was several acres long, and I would spend hours a day of hard labor cutting trees and pulling weeds.-Occasionally, the horses came near to say hello, but they usually sensed I was uninterested and moseyed away feeling pity for me.

These jobs were wake-up calls. They helped me understand it was time for me to reconsider my life path and vision for the future. As a family, we were not about to uproot again, and I knew I wanted to make Mississippi into a place that felt more like we belonged. The hard labor gave me time for meditation and contemplation. I decided to focus my energy on finding employment that could provide me not only with a paycheck, but also a place within the community that would give me a voice and a purpose. It turns out, if you will it into the world with enough faith, wishes can become more than just dreams. I received an answer to my prayers through philanthropy—a field I knew nothing about but instinctively understood I could be good at. This was (and still is) my perfect niche to both support my community and earn a living. I love it. To help those less fortunate is to choose service above self. It's the Mississippi way!

Act Three: Reputation Means Everything

Everyone in the Deep South knows everyone else, whether for good or for ill. If you live in Mississippi, you better not talk shit anywhere in public—not at a local diner, not at church, not at the ball fields surrounded by noise—not anywhere. The second you do, your friend's aunt's second cousin-once-removed will re-serve the tea they just heard you spilling to whoever it was about. The toughest part of trying to fit in is accepting that the good-old-boy network is alive and well. Thank the Lord, I figured that out rather quickly. Now, I'm even part of some of those networks, so don't spill your tea around me either. It takes time to find your place. To be socially successful in any small town, you have to remember that your character and reputation are worth their weight in gold. You will know when you've been accepted, because you will start to notice one of the Deep South's greatest approval gestures—the two-finger salute. Stay on the lookout for this while driving down local, country roads, since it's easy to miss. Everyone notices the details of passing cars, and some even note who is inside as it passes (did I mention that everyone knows everyone down here?) But most people, either because they have lived here too long and have grown complacent, or because they never realized its significance, miss the salute.

If a Mississippian knows and approves of you, they wave. Like all the time, every day. But it's not the same wave used in other parts of the country. The full hand is not required. It's a much more casual gesture, probably because of the frequency it's given—I imagine a full wave would get exhausting after a while. The salute is simply a casual, nonchalant lifting of only two fingers—usually the pointer and middle finger—straight up from the steering wheel as you pass. That's it. You belong. It's like a little symbol of peace and approval. I lived down here for a while before noticing the hand gesture finally directed towards me, and I was ecstatic—I knew I had finally found my place in the Deep South! Clout in the Sip! (On a side note, I have a business idea to manufacture plastic fingers that adhere to the steering wheel so you just finger-salute everyone. *Patent Pending*).

The Encore: A Lesson in Resiliency

No matter how bad it gets down here, southern folks get it done. The true measure of Deep South grit isn't always found in church buildings or on billboards. The best place to experience this is an institution that operates so effectively and efficiently that the U.S. government relies on it as a central source of vital information during hurricanes and other serious emergencies. I'm talking about Waffle House! Make a note: If Waffle House ever closes in your area, run! I used to bag the shit out of this place before moving down south. I was completely ignorant of the vital role Waffle House plays in the wellbeing of southern communities. I still don't have the words to properly explain why it's so important to southern culture. Logically, you can compare it to other breakfast restaurants like Denny's or IHOP, and it would seem like apples to apples. It's not. Somehow, and again I'm not sure exactly how, Waffle House transcends its restaurant identity down here. Put it this way: The stereotype of Mississippians in the rest of the country includes various combinations of laziness, ignorance, poverty, disease or worse. Before you shoot the messenger, I did not invent this stereotype, nor do I subscribe to it. I have occasionally witnessed, however, the common southern mindset of "this is how we've always done it, so that's how we always will." Although, I try to avoid those with this attitude, I make an exception when it comes to Waffle House. If it ain't broke, don't fix it and Waffle House ain't broke. In Mississippi, Waffle House is a state of mind. My goal moving here was to raise a family in a safe place with a community that looks after one other. This kind of security is priceless and something that does not reveal itself via Zillow report. But you can feel the security at any Mississippi Waffle House. Just remember, what happens at Waffle House stays at Waffle House… pass the syrup.

By now, you have probably noticed that the underlying theme of every single place I've lived was struggle. Whether I knew about challenges ahead of time or had to figure out ways around them as they happened, struggle was always present. It always will be. My acceptance of this certainty made life in the thick of it manageable. The expectation of struggle morphed the challenges into adventures in my mind. Each place I lived reshaped my view of the world and myself. With each move, new challenges sharpened my adaptability and chiseled my mindset, teaching me resilience, innovation, and the art of "keep on keeping on."

CALL TO ACTION

Your reputation is judged when eyes are on you. Your character is revealed when they're not. Focus more on character because who you are in the dark defines what shines in the light.

7

GHOSTS AND THE NEW YORK METS

YA GOTTA BELIEVE

"Don't look down on death, but welcome it. It, too, is one of the things required by nature."

—Marcus Aurelius

Ghosts aren't always what people think. They're not transparent floaty things that haunt you—they're burdens we all carry. Old losses. Missed chances. Moments that didn't go our way. And they don't just disappear when the regretful moment passes. Having a job has always been essential in my life, and each job had both pros and cons. Freshmen year of high school, I had a job working at my church. It wasn't a volunteer job once a week like other kids my age, but actual employment for a paycheck. I worked two separate shifts every Saturday and

Sunday. The morning shift included waking up the priests in their bedrooms (yea creepy, I know) and serving them breakfast. I took a break mid-day and then went back to work at night for other duties.

The church was within walking distance of my house, so there was no way my parents were going to wake up that early on weekends to drive me. Daylight savings made it even creepier. During the dark winter months, I began to fear "the car." Every Saturday and Sunday morning around 6 am, as I turned the corner toward the church's large parking lot, I saw a car idling near the entrance. The long walk across that dark lot gave me plenty of time to shit my pants as I approached. Over time, I started concealing a baseball bat up the sleeve of my jacket, always holding my keys ready to open the door as fast as possible. No one, including me, was supposed to be allowed into the auditorium of the church until a certain time, but it was the quickest way into the building, so fuck that. Each morning, I raced past the car, avoiding eye contact, scrambled to unlock the door, then leaped inside while twisting midair to get the door locked back up as quickly as possible. Then every single morning, I peered out the window to watch that car slowly roll out of the lot. Looking back now, I realize that this was actually beyond creepy and very suspicious.

Upon entering the large auditorium, I had to walk through pitch-blackness to the rear of the cavernous room, climb the stairs to the stage, and find the electrical box past a set of curtains. I always felt like I was being watched in the darkness and made a habit of clanking my bat on the floor and folding chairs along the way to relieve tension and hopefully alert anyone hiding behind the curtain to get out before I got there. In hindsight, I have no idea why I never brought a flashlight. I guess I was a stupid kid. I was definitely paranoid, but you have to admit, it was such an eerie situation for a kid. The panel was on the right side, just past the curtains that were always drawn over the stage. Many times, I swung that bat so hard while climbing the stairs that I almost tore the curtain down. If anyone was ever hiding there, he or she would have been hit. After I was sure the coast was clear, I threw open the power box and clicked all switches at once. Illumination. Relief. Nothing ever seemed as bad when the lights were on.

Most of the time, the creepiest part of the morning was the car (stalker). One morning, though, something even scarier happened. I didn't see the figure on the stage at first. I was probably too panicked leaping through the door and getting it locked. But after the stalker left, I turned around, straining my eyes toward the opposite end of the auditorium, and something seemed different. I looked down for a moment to put my keys away while my eyes adjusted to the darkness, and when I looked up again, there she was. An older woman, shaggily dressed, with eyes the size of small moons. She was staring right at me… staring right through me. I felt the intensity of her glare clear across the auditorium. I squeezed my eyes tight for a second, then looked back up. She was gone. Damn. I still had to turn on the lights and do my job. I'm no longer ashamed to admit, I very seriously considered running. Then, I thought about my paycheck and decided to pretend it was all in my imagination. It could have been. It was incredibly dark. After getting the lights on, I was supposed to open the church building, which was adjacent to the auditorium. I was also pressed for time because I still had to wake up the priests, cook them some kind of breakfast, and set the altar up for the day's first mass. Decision made, I braced myself (and the bat) and plowed forward.

I got through the auditorium and upon entering the church, I located the light switches in the sacristy. This was a small waiting room where the priest donned his robes and the altar boys waited for their duties to begin (and sometimes sneaked a sip or two of wine before mass). Lights on–

check. It was time to unlock the church. To do this, I had to pass by the confessionals. One "box" was where the priest sat during confession; another was a private booth with curtains for sinners who wanted to remain anonymous. The third "box" was a tiny room with two chairs used to repent face to face with the priest. Way too many hiding places for creepers.

I violently swung each door opened with my bat and prayed they were empty. All clear, thank God. Most of the time, they were. Once, however, I found a passed out homeless person and ran like hell. My next obstacle was the church vestibule, which I also had to unlock. Over the time I worked for the church, I occasionally found people sleeping in there, or worse, staring at me from the front door wanting in. I never knew what to do. Unlock the door? Run? Usually, I kept the door locked until they got the point. It all depended on their eyes. If they looked crazy, I kept it locked. On this day, the vestibule was empty.

After unlocking everything and reminding the priest to prepare for mass in twenty minutes, it was time to set up the altar. My job included setting out chalices and holy cloths and then lighting the altar candles. I usually enjoyed this part. Standing on the altar overlooking the church and auditorium felt somehow majestic. After the lady started appearing, though, the experience became less pleasant. Yes, I saw her again. Many times. That day, as I peered out across the church pews, there she was… .same old lady, same bulging eyes. It was the beginning of multiple sightings. Sometimes she was seated in the right front row, sometimes in the last row. I still can't get those eyes out of my head, gaping with a look of both terror and evil that pierced my soul. It really was way too much for a fifteen-year-old to handle. My parents didn't agree. And I never mentioned it to the priests. Yes, of course, I now realize I should have spoken up. Like my failure to bring a flashlight to the dark auditorium, I again have no idea why I kept the appearance of that lady a secret. For whatever reason, I stuck it out and kept the job. The lady never spoke or bothered me, so I never bothered her. In the end, a huge part of my development and maturity came from surviving that job. After that, I knew for a fact, and from a very young age, that it was up to me (and only me) to face my fears and walk tall. Figuring shit out on my own is a lesson that has helped me make my way through the world. It also taught me the value of bringing fresh underwear into creepy situations.

Unfortunately, this was not my only possibly supernatural experience. Another recurrent event from my childhood happened at my home on Long Island. We had a loft where my younger brother and I slept. It was a decent size, so we weren't that crammed together, and my bed was close to the window. Not sure what triggered me to wake up, but I always did. It usually happened in the early mornings, near dawn. I startled awake from deep sleep, then heard feet shuffling outside my window. It sounded like someone walking off the sidewalk and up to the side of the house. The house was two stories high, but after the shuffling sound, I always sensed someone (or something) floating right outside the window, staring at me. Imagination? Maybe. But my absolute terror prevented me from opening my eyes to look. After what always seemed like at least an hour, the sense slowly faded, as though it was drifting back down to the ground. Only moments later, I would hear the footsteps walking away and breathe a sigh of relief… which never lasted, because the footsteps always returned. They sounded almost like the pitter-patter of a mid-sized animal as I clearly heard them enter the front door of our house and pad up the stairs. The floor of the stairs was wooden (no carpet to muffle sound), so I heard every detail of the "thing's" ascent and into the loft where we slept. And then, every single time, it padded right up to the side of my bed. I kept my eyes glued shut during these frightening episodes, but this only heightened all my other senses could as it stared at me, only about an inch from my face. I didn't have any pets. I was pretty sure ghosts were quiet. Whatever it was, it would then turn around and exit the house the same way it came. Weird, right? But it gets even weirder because, like clockwork, the sound of footsteps always came right back from the side of the house. Again, I felt it peering through my bedroom window before lowering back down, heading back into the house, up the stairs, and close to my face. On some nights, this happened over and over. Every single time, I just froze—completely paralyzed—never even considering screaming for my brother, who was usually snoring ten feet away, or for my parents just down the hall. Most times, I ended the experience by finally passing out from terror. In the mornings, I simply woke up and got the day going like nothing ever happened. I was always secretly thankful that the morning's ghost encounter was over, but I knew no one would ever believe me, so I stayed quiet.

These experiences changed me. I believe in "other" beings: whether those beings are ghosts, spirits, aliens or something else, I have no idea—but I still believe. I found out much later that someone once died in the house we lived in; nothing murderous or suspicious, just an average death. There was a time in my life this would have terrified me, but not anymore. The scary thing about the idea of ghosts isn't whether or not they're real. The scary thing about ghosts is the idea they represent. Fear. Mystery. Mortality. The quiet sense that a secret, unknown separate existence is happening in real time in a way we don't understand. Realizing where this fear comes from has made me less afraid. I now know that the sooner humans confront our fears, the better off we are. The fact is, there is some weird shit out there that we may never understand. Pretending it doesn't exist only makes it seem scarier. It's probably best to go ahead and accept the unknown or unexplained as a normal part of life. That way these encounters may still be weird, but they won't make you paralyzed and helpless with terror.

If I'm being honest, those mornings left a mark on me for a while. For years I hated the dark. I hated the quiet moments when your mind has too much room to wander. I learned much too early in life that fear doesn't need facts: it just needs imagination. But I also learned that fear loses its grip when you keep moving through it. Every weekend, I continued to unlock those doors, to walk straight into that darkness, and to turn on the lights. I didn't know it then, but those simple acts would become a pattern for the rest of my life.

Speaking of irrational beliefs, I've also had an unflinching faith in the New York Mets my entire life. People tell me this is not good for my soul, but when you grow up on Long Island, you don't think of the Mets as a baseball team. They are a religion—a dysfunctional, heartbreaking, beautiful religion. I loved them from birth. Still do. And loving the Mets means learning disappointment early. It means believing in something that rarely rewarded you. It means showing up no matter what, holding onto hope, win or lose, and letting that hope shape, rather than shatter, you. Their slogan is simple: *Ya Gotta Believe*, which is either inspiring or insane. Either way, I'll keep believin'.

Many teachings of Stoicism suggest that belief in something unseen isn't about imagination or fantasy. It's about endurance. It's about accepting that you have no control over life's scoreboard, because all you can really control is how steady you stay during the game. The Mets taught me that life doesn't always provide closure. Sometimes it gives you extra innings, but often only offers a September collapse. Sure, the occasional miracle has happened, but even then, your role is the same: You're still left sitting there, beer in hand, heart exposed, just watching. That's the Mets... and the human condition. Ghosts, baseball, death, hope—it's all the same stage, just different backdrops. Marcus Aurelius wasn't telling us to be numb to the mysteries of the unknown. He was telling us to face them with honesty. Death is coming. Disappointment is coming. So, don't waste your life pretending it doesn't exist. Believe. But believe with discipline. Believe without attachment. And when the season breaks your heart—again—remember: You're still here, and that's the win.

CALL TO ACTION

The unknown isn't something to fear—it's something to walk toward. Every life has dark rooms, unanswered questions, and moments you want to freeze. Don't! Turn the lights on. Curiosity, courage, and a little belief are the only tools you need.

8

THOMAS GUIDES

AND THE MAP OF LIFE

"All men make mistakes, but a good man yields when he knows his course is wrong and repairs the evil. The only crime is pride."

—Sophocles

When we didn't have weekend sports, we sometimes found ourselves on the dreaded Murphy family vacation. Think of a discounted version of the Griswolds without Wally World. One of our favorite spots was a lake house community just down the Jersey Turnpike. It was fun except when the home's owners showed up drunk with friends to party. Then, it was weird. The kids who lived around the lake were a mixed bag. Some were cool, but others were flat out juvenile delinquents. It was definitely a diverse crowd. I once met a kid there who had allegedly been brutally molested. When the vacation was over, I remember looking back through the car window as we hightailed it out of there. The kid just stood there in the middle of the street waving until we were completely out of sight. Very sad. I hope the rumors about his situation were false.

On each Murphy vacation, I wondered again who Thomas was and why we kept a textbook-sized book of maps with his name on it in our car. The maps covered every major city in the United States. Whoever he was, God bless him for his navigational prowess; it gave me the freedom to thoroughly explore Hollywood in the early stages of my entertainment career. There were times when I spent the better part of my week in a car driving around town to drop off scripts, deliver rough cuts of movies, and transport gifts (bribes) both warranted and unwarranted. I learned where the popular celebrities lived, who their managers and agents were, and the temperaments of infamous producers who enjoyed acting like egotistical assholes just to fit the stereotype.

As I worked my way up through industry ranks, speed was a necessity. Hollywood big wigs were not known for patience. The grunt work had to be done, and I couldn't afford to get lost or waste time stuck in traffic. Back then, drivers proved their navigational skills by reading maps; it was a rite of passage used to determine whether a person was headed in the right direction (pun intended) or completely clueless.

As a practitioner of Stoicism, I do try to swallow my pride, when possible, but I'll admit a bit of a big head when I remember my mad map skills. Gen X was the last generation on the planet to grow up with no cell phones or internet. Cry me a river, I know. Despite the role it played to help shape both the character and success of countless generations, map navigation is becoming a lost art. Most young drivers have never experienced the feeling of true disorientation, but the possibility of getting terribly lost was a regular concern for everyone who came before them. It was just part of life and exploration! No phones, no fear. We regularly practiced the art of diplomatically by stopping to ask for directions.

Okay, that was a lie. Men of all ages, to this day, will not lower their standards to ask for directions. Wives, girlfriends, and moms, however, did practice this art.

Although Thomas Maps were my personal favorite, there were other brands of various shapes and sizes. Some were large paper sheets, approximately the size of a kitchen table, which were folded in a way that required a PhD in origami to master. Improper map unfolding or refolding was a well-known cause of chaos, rage, and even an occasional divorce. It was also well-known that no matter how much we prepped for any trip, there always came a time for the map. It was either that or we had to pull over to ask for directions, which (as you know) was only used as a last resort. Maps first. So, when the time of unfolding arrived, we silenced the radio, ended conversations, and the car filled with anxiety as thick as gaseous fumes. It felt like sitting in a circle with an unpinned hand grenade… who wants to hold it?

During the times (mistakes) that I volunteered (was forced by my family) to navigate, I usually managed to make the tension worse. As you may have guessed by now, I was a troublemaker, and family excursions were a bad time for my wiseass tricks. Once, after the family car was loaded down and we had been driving for hours, I was forced in charge of the map. After finally realizing we were not on the right path but failing to figure out where we went wrong or how to correct it, I was refolding the map in defeat (probably incorrectly) and tensions inside the car were at an all-time high. As we added up the time we had lost going the wrong direction, and family tempers had reached the boiling point, I decided to blurt out "oh shit, you know what we forgot?" I loved doing this. It didn't matter if we were barreling down a crowded side street or (as we were this time) speeding along a parkway full of traffic, my dad's first reaction was always to slam on the brakes and swerve almost all the way off the road in panic. That was my cue to say, "Just kidding," always stupidly expecting laughter and approval from my two brothers in the back seat. No idea why I always expected this. It never came, since they were always too terrified from the near fiery death experience. What did always come my way was the flat of my dad's ring-fingered hand against the back of my head. Hard. Usually followed by a long period of utter silence.

At the time, I thought those head slaps were just part of the Murphy family comedy routine. Looking back, they were formative experiences. My dad had zero tolerance for arrogance. If you screwed up, he expected you to own it, fix it, and move on. Pride didn't impress him, and neither did bad judgment. Competence did. I didn't realize it then, but without a word my dad taught me a philosophy that Stoicism would later confirm—mistakes are inevitable, but consequences are a certainty, and refusing to admit your faults can be much more damaging than a slap to the back of the head.

After Dad calmed down, he finally admitted he needed to pull over and ask for directions. The fact that a man was asking for directions is probably one of the main reasons this story stands out so vividly in my memories. It was a momentous occasion and a testament to just how lost we were. For any non-Gen X readers, I should point out that this doesn't mean asking Siri. It means that our family had to confront the only remaining, last-resort navigational option available to us… physically pulling the car off the road into an unknown area of the world to ask the closest random person for directions. This was a tricky sport, even back then, and one that not everyone could pull off. We learned pretty quickly which type of person we were… either the ones who did the talking, or the ones who kept their mouths shut and listened. Back then it was not at all weird to ask someone out loud, window rolled down, "where the hell am I? And where the hell do I need to go to get out of this spot?" But you also had to be cordial, direct, and listen (not my specialty). Asking someone to repeat the directions, or worse, asking the stranger to explain more detail, could very well lead to total disregard, a simple "fuck off," or even a beer bottle to the windshield. In my case, at least when I rode with my dad, my window conversations usually ended in a second slap to the back of the head. Disclaimer: I deserved (almost) every head slap I received.

Despite the independence that non-technological navigation taught me, I don't judge modern kids for their navigational challenges. I'd be a fool if I didn't acknowledge that it's a different world now with undeniable limitations when it comes to approaching strangers. Getting lost can actually be dangerous. Driving with no GPS? Going for a walk without a phone? Good luck. It has become risky, even for the brave hearted. But it couldn't hurt to occasionally pocket the tech and feel the world out without so many guardrails. Learn your way around with your eyes and mind, and you could just become more confident in your wayward abilities without having to endure my dad's trademark head slap. It's a win-win!

I grew up learning that mistakes are okay (or at least expected), so I may as well "fuck it and give it a shot," whatever the "it" may be. I've carried this attitude with me, and it makes me braver each time. A recent example of how I live with a "fuck it," attitude is when I was visiting Vietnam for business. I had, or thought I had, discovered a local clothing store online that sold knock-off hipster brands for a fraction of the U.S. (authentic product) price. I had seen stuff like this before while in China (again for work) and had picked up some apparel for my sons without any issues.

I guess this past success made me cocky. This time, however, testing my street smarts and attitude on an international level didn't work out the way I planned.

Before visiting the shop, I decided that going off into an unknown area of a foreign country should be done during daylight hours. It's lucky I did, because the trip to this pirate clothing store sent me to parts of Hanoi that, let's just politely say, I wasn't planning to visit. When the driver arrived in the deserted alley of a seedy, rundown "neighborhood," I got out and quickly knew it was a mistake. I turned to get back in the car, but without hesitation or even stopping his cell phone conversation, the driver was already speeding off leaving me alone with my regret. *Man, did I really fuck this up or what?* I just stood there for a minute, all alone in a secluded alley, so far away from home. As reality sank in that I was in a completely unfamiliar part of the world with no cellphone reception and a swiftly draining battery, I decided that my naive images of a loving family enjoying bootleg apparel would have to be put on the backburner. As helplessness sank in, I was starting to wonder if I would ever even see them again. As if triggered by that feeling of hopelessness, the Gen-X part of me woke up, stretched its badass muscles, and said, "Bitchin'… another challenge! Let's get 'er done!" See what I mean? Fuck it. Time to put away my pride, embrace the mistake, and re-direct the hopelessness to solutions. Looking around, I understood one thing… way over "there" was the district of Hanoi that I needed to get back to, and I was separated from that by a large lake. The first thing I did was turn my cellphone off to keep any battery power available in case of a real emergency. Next, I walked and walked and walked. I walked through scanty villages and rundown streets full of young students eating dinner on the sidewalks while yelling at me. Still no idea what they were yelling. Eventually, feeling exhausted and beaten down, I looked up and recognized a hotel sign just up the road. I was still very far away from my destination, so I entered the desolate lobby and looked around for someone who may be willing to help. It felt absolutely magical to discover that the somewhat-confused young desk clerk, by the grace of God, had a phone with a translation app! After only a few minutes, she began to understand my situation and called for a car to drive me home. Although it took another hour for the car to arrive, and I had to walk another mile to find it, I eventually made it safely back to my hotel well past midnight. The hotel lobby was desolate, but I can't even describe how refreshing it was to walk through that door and into safety after being so alone and scared, knowing that I had found my own way out of the situation. The moment was invigorating, or proud, or metamorphic, or cathartic, I don't really know. But it was awesome, whatever it was, and the feeling mattered because it changed me into something more than I was. The ice-cold beers in my hotel mini fridge were a very close second to that feeling.

What surprised me most about the experience wasn't that I found my way back. It was how calm I felt afterward. Years earlier, getting lost like that would have sent me into full panic mode. But somewhere along the path of my life, I must have learned that mistakes don't predict the certainty of doom. They're just a detour. And if you keep walking long enough, most detours eventually reconnect with the main path.

Somewhere between the Thomas Guides of youth and that dark alley in Hanoi, I realized something important about the direction of life. It's complicated and rarely navigated without wrong turns. I guess Sophocles had it right: The only real crime is pride, because pride keeps you lost by preventing you from moving forward. Wisdom is gained from sucking up that pride and admitting mistakes in order to find your way through to a solution. I understand now that Gen X wasn't unfortunate because of our struggles. We were lucky to have had no choice but struggle. These challenges have molded a unique understanding of mistakes, and most of us are able to recognize them as natural parts of life instead of personal or character-defining failures. In the end, the glitches and foldouts of our youth weren't so much obstacles, as they were blueprints for blazing trails through the world.

CALL TO ACTION

Calculated risk-taking will compound your success. Try going for a drive somewhere new without using your GPS. See if you can find your way back home on your own. The experience may teach you to navigate roads, but the real lesson will be the moment you discover that getting lost isn't failure. It's practice. Just a natural part of the learning process.

9

CYO DANCES AND SWEET SIXTEENS

"True happiness is to enjoy the present, without anxious dependence upon the future."

—Seneca

Growing up, the boys of my neighborhood were blessed (or cursed) with an all-girls' high school just down the street. Around the time my hormones started controlling my appearance and "style," I attended an all-boys private school where I was forced to wear a tie starting in kindergarten. Like most kids there, my only opportunities to establish my identity was at recess, on weekends, or during summer holidays. My first attempt to publicly define my unique style, for better or for worse, came in the form of a trench coat. I'm pretty sure I owned the only trenchcoat in the neighborhood, and no, it was not

Columbine-esque. I thought of it as part Lloyd Dobler from "Say Anything", and part J Crew. But honestly, one of the main reasons I wore it all the time was because I could hide a six-pack in all the pockets… or at least I thought I could. There was that one time I got cocky before a Midnight Oil show at the Felt Forum (MSG) and tried to fit an entire case of beer. Hysterically, I couldn't fit through the turnstile to get in. After pawning off two cans to the security guard, he let me pass.

Testosterone, teenage angst, and unpredictable bursts of youthful energy are a funny combo, and CYO (Catholic Youth Organization) dances created a perfect storm for those emotions to collide outside of school and, unfortunately, right in front of the girls I was so desperate to impress. The dances were on Friday nights, but the obligatory veiled threats and make-out plans surrounding them began as early as Monday. Most times, neither blossomed into reality. Most of the kids at my boy's school attended the dances, since we were the only ones invited. Public school want-to-be tough guys sometimes stood in the street looking down into the cafeteria, creating thug-like silhouettes against the windows of the building. Me and my gang of boys could never tell who exactly was up there from their distorted shadows, so evening included a litany of stampedes up the stairs (with chaperones chasing) to investigate the threats. Often, it was just our own older brothers teasing us. This was faux-macho junior high shit at its finest, always some sort of drama.

For me, the worst drama at one of these dances began when an unnamed, but very prominent figure of our community (and dear friend of my parents) saw me acting like a jackass and decided to intervene. He grabbed my arm in the middle of the dance floor, spun me around, and accused me quite loudly of being drunk. Of course I lied. I even accused him of lying. Bad move. He snatched opened my trench coat and found four Budweiser bottles, still ice cold, in my interior pockets. He was so violent during his search that one bottle actually fell out, hit the ground, and shattered all over the dance floor. As A-Ha's "Take on Me," continued to blare from the cafeteria speakers, I stood there, frozen in humiliation, as the staff turned on the house lights to clear the hall and mop up the mess. There was no way out of this one except the exit door. Naturally, I was banned from future CYO dances.

I retrospect, the public reprimand wasn't just an embarrassing situation. Somehow, it also made me feel small. Less. Ashamed. It was the first time I fully comprehended the magnitude of foolishness I was able to feel. It took a very public humiliation in front of the people I wanted to impress most in the world to realize (finally) that cleverness can dramatically backfire and that pride only escalates bad situations and makes fools of us all. I was able to laugh about it later, but standing there in the moment, heart pounding and panic threatening to eat me alive, I just wanted the floor to swallow me whole. Thankfully, that lashing stuck with me, and not just during future dances (non-CYO, of course). It became a lifelong reminder that humility isn't optional if I wanted to navigate life without tripping over my own ego.

As time passed and cafeteria-style break dancing got old, coupled with my permanent ban from CYO dances, my friends and I shifted interest to Sweet Sixteen parties. The girls we knew back then were usually very selective about which boys to hang out with, or at least they were wise enough to think twice about inviting certain individuals to their big Sweet 16 parties. Many of the birthday girls still disapproved of my friend group, not only because of the dance "incident." We were troublemakers. But they needed at least *some* boys at their events, so they usually rolled the dice. Although yes, I was mischievous, ultimately the innocent face of "Murph" usually earned me some undeserved forgiveness. I got the invite every time. Each Saturday for about six months, there was an epic party, and it only took my crew of troublemakers about a minute to concoct a brilliant pregaming scam before the Sweet Sixteen season began. Everyone threw in a couple of bucks from our paper routes to buy a case of beer the day before the party and stash it in the bushes somewhere. The next day, we used one of the moms' wrapping paper to make it look like a birthday gift. One of our parents carpooled us to the event (sidenote: carpools were common in the 70s and 80s), so if your mom or dad wasn't driving, you took credit for bringing "the gift" for Krista, Teresa, Patti, Laura, Carrie….etc. etc.

Sometimes the act of pulling a case of beer from the bushes that you stashed the night before, or the process of asking an old, salty dog to buy you beer, or maybe even stealing a bottle of hard liquor from one of the parents created an even bigger buzz than the alcohol. Here's where Stoicism fits the story: Whether teenage Murph knew it or not (and no, I'm not condoning illegal activity in pursuit of a buzz), the feeling was always deeper than the buzz. The feeling came from our ability to completely engage in the moment. It came from embracing opportunities as they presented, without building our entire lives around chasing perfection. Our expectations were to anticipate the events of life and decide to make the best of them. We created moments we wanted to experience from what we had, rather than expecting the magical moments to come to us. It was intentional. Sometimes our intentions didn't work out the way we planned, and we embraced that too as opportunities to look for other moments to create. The excitement of life came from the understanding that pleasure is meant to be a seasoning of life, rather than the main course, or worse, an escape from life's realities. The act of carving out unlikely (and even sometimes forbidden) pleasures within the more mundane processes of life is powerful and transformative… even if the methods we used were sometimes not completely healthy or responsible.

The Seneca quote at the beginning of this essay wasn't telling you to stop living. It is a warning against outsourcing your happiness to the next perfect moment, the next party invitation, the next "like," or the next approval. Your life can be lived with a constant "buzz," by simply recognizing the value of everyday moments and refusing to discount or undervalue the simplicity of daily life. By embracing and engaging intentionally with these simple moments, you are taking the reins of your own happiness. Rather than simply enduring the mundane moments of life as a wall-flower or observer, we become more joyful by intentionally interacting and imposing our own will to each experience. This is literally the spice of life. Oh—and never attend a party without a gift. Manners, baby!

CALL TO ACTION

Courage leads to confidence. This month, intentionally perform one socially brave action without using alcohol, nostalgia, or performance as a crutch. Show up as yourself—awkward, imperfect, awake, and fully present. That's where the growth happens.

10

SALT BAGELS

"It is not the man who has too little, but the man who craves more, that is poor."

—Seneca

Stoicism emphasizes the importance of daily rituals to live virtuously and grow personally. Stoic rituals are intentional, not rigid, and help people ground themselves in these timeless virtues. They can help people develop traits like patience, courage, gratitude, and a buffer against stress. I sure could've used some of these rituals back in the day when my mom sent me out for bagels. The bagel shop was the most beloved, revered, and cherished shop in our community and, fresh out of the oven, their product was a religious experience. I knew my place in the shop and was careful not to ask them to butter the bagels when it was super crowded. That was called a spit bagel. Saturday mornings in my house were a crapshoot regarding breakfast options, but the cornucopia of cartoons was plentiful. *Smurfs, Planet of the Apes, Looney Tunes* and *Flintstones. Tom and Jerry, The Jetsons* and even *Hong Kong Phooey* held marquee status in my household. Most of the time, only my two brothers and I got up early and we had to fistfight over who got the last of the Captain Crunch. The loser was stuck with scraps of Raisin Bran and no milk. My oldest brother used to put orange juice in his cereal. Disgusting, but efficient. Considering the usual breakfast options, it's easy to understand how excited we got on the rare occasions my parents took us out for bagels.

"Get dressed and get in the car," my parents called, and for once we ran to obey. The setting was always the same at the shop–a line of about a dozen townsfolk, all eyeballing multiple levels of racks with variations of bagels in cages. I didn't give two shits about fancy flavored bagels, "everything" bagels, or (possibly the worst bagel option ever created) cinnamon raisin. Hell no. My eyes stayed glued to the lower left metal basket and those motherfucking salt bagels!! Every night my dog drools like a fool watching us eat dinner, which is pathetic… but what's even more pathetic is that right now, writing about this topic, my mouth is frothing just thinking about those bagels. New York water, baby!!!!

Getting the bagels wasn't a simple process. Before ordering, we had to assess the pecking order and the speed of the line. It was necessary to gauge any unfinished beefs between patrons standing in line that may have carried tension over from the night before. In other words, the line always moved as fast as possible, but there was usually plenty of time and opportunities for drama while in the shop. The only time of peace in the bagel shop was early on Sundays when everyone was still in their church clothes. The fighting, cursing and mean looks still simmered, but temporarily paused for that morning only.

After getting our bearings, we were fools if we didn't keep our eyes and ears opened for snippets of juicy gossip, since the bagel shop was sometimes as informative as a confessional box. We also used the shop as an opportunity to occasionally air our own grievances. Once we arrived at the front of the line, however, our family knew that we better shut the fuck up and know what we were ordering and how many, or we would be leaving empty handed. That was always the first question they barked at us.

"How many?"

"*Two* bagels?" They asked, visibly judging the small order as they threw them in a small bag reserved for paupers. For an order of a dozen bagels, we always got thirteen, and they put them in a medium brown sack like a gift straight from God. I've seen customers order several dozen, and the workers busted out the paper version of an army-issued duffel bag to launch all those yeast circles into. Whatever we ordered, though, we remembered the three cardinal rules of the bagel shop: Decide what you want before you get to the front of the line, do not hesitate to answer when they ask what you want, and speak loudly and clearly… probably best to just yell it if you're nervous. Then get the fuck out of the way for other customers. I think Cicero himself would have respected the process.

As an older kid, sometimes my parents sent me out for the bagels. Most of the time I got the order right. Occasionally when we went, they were out of hot salties, and I would be stuck with a plain bagel. That sucked, but my childhood nickname (besides "Murph") was "Meat and a Roll" (more on that later), so at least I wasn't the picky kid in the family. Heading out with my medium-sized bag, I kept an eye out for anyone interesting still waiting in line. I once saw an eggy local, allegedly undefeated in bar fights, throw a guy straight through the front glass window of the shop because he complained about the long line! Strong Island, baby!

On a lucky day, I was allowed to order two bagels and devoured the first one before I even got home. Most people sliced them up, put butter or lox or fucking cream cheese on them, or sometimes even bacon, lettuce, and tomato. Not me. I grabbed the bagel on my way out the door and gnawed it straight from the bag like a fucking rat in Times Square. I always ate the second bagel at home while watching my favorite cartoon–*Fat Albert*, "Hey hey hey!"

So, why am I telling you all this? Because it all comes down to habits. Rituals. Routines. There was a process to the occasion, and although this process was sometimes comically violent, the habit and reward usually made me feel… alright. Better than alright. Secure. Getting Sunday bagels was such a simple act for a simple reward, but the process sometimes kept my spirits up well into the next day. Habits can be like that. Over a lifetime, habits will come and go and ultimately, it's up to us to decipher between the habits which forward our lives and the ones holding us back. I try to lose the anchors as soon as they're identified, but that's not always easy to do. Bad habits, if left to take root, can compound to create a terrible life. Since we only have one life, it's probably best to maximize the stoke. To decide which habits are best left behind, I try to notice and appreciate the processes of my life that fill my soul, and the ones that seem to drain it.

In my case, the act of giving to others fills my soul. It makes me feel complete. Fulfilled. Somehow taller than I was before. Realizing this, I took a deep dive into the world of philanthropy and found a way to turn it into a career. After this, I felt like my life still wasn't busy enough, so I served as the director of a boarding school for seventh to twelfth grade boys. I can see myself in every one of them and I've come to the decision that, in a dorm full of boys and young men, the word habit doesn't land the way philosophers think it will. Their brains aren't hardwired yet to see the long arc of things to come. Because of this, I've learned not to even try to teach them to use good habits for philosophical purposes. Instead, I build an environment where good habits can be formed whether they understand their importance or not.

I think ancient Stoics would appreciate the strategy. They seemed to understand that people rarely change behavior based on speeches or lectures. Usually people change lifestyles because of repetition, circumstances, or structure. I think of it as using a road with rails until the traveler learns to steer without crashing. Eventually, adulthood will reveal the quieter truth behind good habits: the big moments in life are just the scoreboard. The habits they created were the practices that enabled the wins.

On a side note, I consider most of the Sunday cartoons we watched back then to be kid-friendly, even if some seemed a bit off color compared to modern standards. But there's no way that *Fat Albert* or *Hong Kong Phooey* would have survived the modern content apocalypse. With so many channels to choose from lately, many with upfront warnings and disclaimers, it's almost impossible find a show with cartoon characters that are edgy or experience real conflict. When I grew up, you just threw on a channel and started watching. On the other hand, I also remember laughing my ass off while watching movies with my parents when, out of left field, the show added a random sexual innuendo or some other kind of adult content. I laughed more at the speed of my parents, than the content, as they jumped up to change the channel or lower the sound to shield me from something I had already heard at school. It was hysterical. In general, though, this new era of television has too many yellow brick roads and cotton candy dreams.

CALL TO ACTION

Don't forget the struggle, don't forget the streets. Pick one small ritual this week that grounds you—morning coffee, a walk, a meal, a phone call. Do it with full presence. Don't forget the streets, but don't live trapped in them either. Having trouble finding a ritual that grounds you? Go back to your roots. What made you feel like your life was structured and safe as a kid? Focus on that.

11

A DRINK—PART ONE

"Drunkenness is nothing but voluntary madness."

—Seneca

Fortunately (or unfortunately) drinking has been a part of my life since about seventh grade. My dad rarely drank. In fact, once, as he drove me home from the hospital after getting my stomach pumped (don't try to down a bottle of gin in twenty minutes) he mentioned he had only gotten drunk once while in the Army. Back then I didn't believe him, but now I totally do. I also finally understand that limited alcohol consumption is not a badge of shame, but a mark of character. Drinking shouldn't be about bravado. A glass or two of red wine with dinner can be a comforting pleasure after a day of work. I'll repeat for emphasis, *after work…* meaning all daily responsibilities have been completed and the family has been thoroughly provided for. In this case, the drink becomes the seasoning of life and not the main course. Not survival.

I know what you're thinking and yes, there have been many times I thought about quitting, but usually while nursing a severe hangover or foggy memories of the previous night. The truth is, drinking was a major part of the culture and traditions where I grew up, and in my case, moderation is a more reasonable option than quitting cold turkey. I've witnessed countless disasters in high school and college where the token male or female consumed way too much alcohol either showing off or simply not knowing their limits. It never ended well, and they always managed to suck the life right out of the party. Low key, that was me at times. As an adult, I thankfully now have the ability to step back and genuinely dissect my actions, behavior, and motivations for drinking more objectively. It has helped me understand the parameters I personally need around alcohol, as well as the consequences and reputation that come with ignoring those boundaries. Moral of the story–when you drink, don't be a jackass.

I remember drinking at junior high and high school parties. I was popular with the jocks, the dirtbags, and the older kids, but few people saw me ducking off into dimly lit backyards, parking lots, or the woods guzzling alcohol to quell my social anxiety. I drank to numb my worry about who was there, why I was there, and what would happen before the night ended. I drank to kill the stress of thinking about whether a girl or girls I liked would come, what to do if random guys that liked or didn't like me started trouble, and any other anxieties my racing mind could overthink. I usually drained at least two beers before walking in the door just to be "Murph," and I always brought a six-pack of beer (Schmidt's!!) with me to get through the mingling. I had to. Not for fun… for armor. What my young mind never realized was that alcohol was serving as both a tool and a crutch. Have I learned my lesson? I firmly believe that the addict must want to quit or it's never going to happen. This is true, because I've seen it in others, and in myself. Sure, it would be great if I never drank again, but I don't really want to quit. So, I try to set reasonable goals and avoid extremes when possible. This measurable success allows me to remain guilt-free in canceling any thoughts of going dry… for now. I realize, of course, that this may be a flawed philosophy, and I will eventually need to take it to another level. After all, to be truly superior in all that we do, we should probably lose the drink completely. Sad, but true.

Alcohol will be a battle for some and a non-issue for others. It hardly seems fair. In life, the bartender often puts another beer down in front of you unrequested. They know you want another one. It's up to us to cut the supply. Stoics believe that virtue means acting with clarity. If another drink changes your character, then stop. That may be a tough shot to swallow, but it's ultimately on us decide when to put on the brakes.

Long before I ever considered putting on my drinking brakes, I landed one of my first real jobs. Everyone has a dream job. Oddly enough, this is the story of mine (at least as a teenager). Of course, it involved drinking. As a young adult, I didn't have a choice about whether or not to get a job. It was not optional. As a Gen X kid, my parents were too busy to find a job for me, so I knew I had to figure it out myself. I was ecstatic when I landed a job as a stock boy/can recycler/bottle counter/delivery grunt/walk-in connoisseur for the local beverage center in my town. The business had a small shop up front where customers could buy beer, soda, mixers, or a cold drink from the walk-in fridge. Out back, there was a warehouse where all the pallets of beer, soda, and kegs were kept. Back in the day, kegs were giant—

like the size of outdoor garbage cans. There was also a basement for cases of tonics, promotional cardboard cut-outs, and other random junk. I was only 16 years old.

Around this time, recycling was becoming a big deal, and most people actually tried to recycle shit as much as they could. It was mostly cans and bottles, and part of my job was to process and sort them. I had about a half dozen tall bins for each distributor's empties… Coca Cola, Pepsi, Anheuser Busch (before getting sold to foreigners), Coors, and other imports. Customers got back five cents per empty bottle or can, no questions asked… and I mean *no* questions. People brought in garbage bags full of unwashed cans, and I had to personally pull them from the bags, count them, throw them into the respective bins, and then write a number on a yellow sticky note. Just a number. I did this while they stood there and waited. The quicker I counted, the quicker they got the fuck away from me. Sometimes I'd reach into a garbage bag infested with maggots and stale liquids. It was gross. Who knows what kinds of bacteria-infused diseases I was exposed to. Some people were much kinder (at least, cleaner) and more organized. In these cases, I usually added another twenty or so to their sticky note totals. One guy came in every Saturday morning. He never said a word, just dropped off two empty six-packs of Michelob light which were placed carefully back into the cardboard six-pack holder. Then one day, out of thin air, he began adding just one more—a single "Mich-lite" bottle—bringing his Saturday totals to thirteen. Every time. Thirteen. After I passed him his sticky note, he always grabbed two cold sixers from the fridge and checked out. I always wondered where that thirteenth bottle came from. Never did ask.

One racket I pulled from time to time was having a friend walk in with a large garbage bag half-filled with two-liter soda bottles. To the untrained eye, the bag looked like it was bursting at the seams, but it was mostly air. I "counted them," pretending there were a hundred beer cans in the bag with the bottles. Again, the only accounting used by the cashier was my sticky note, which was ex-changed for a cash refund(a $5 refund per bag!). Eventually it became obvious that my friends weren't actually bringing in 200 cans per week, and that racket went kapoosh.

If you are wondering why I loved this job so much, one of the reasons was the alcohol. Although I was underage, if I worked hard, my bosses were generous with alcohol at the end of the night. Meaning, I could buy (I mean they could buy) a sixer for me, sometimes a case, or occasionally even a keg! I was King Shit on Saturday nights when I rolled up to the usual hang out spot with ice cold beer that wasn't stolen from a parent's refrigerator!

At the end of each workday, my last responsibility was restocking the walk-in for the next day. During the summer, the work was brutal, but stashing cold beer between kegs and guzzling them between hauling in cases made it bearable. Thinking back now, I can still taste every one of those beers. Dinkelacker's and Budweiser nips were the best!

That wasn't even the highlight of the job. The part that made it a dream job was when I got to tag along with the older employees for deliveries. Not older as in the kind who try to take advantage of kids in the delivery truck (you know the type), but just regular guys, maybe in their mid-twenties. The guys who are destined to be lifers in the beverage industry but still had at least a little spirit left in them. Some of these deliveries were standard, like delicatessens or 7-Elevens. But every now and then, I got help out with deliveries to the local strip clubs and dive bars. The bars were fun because each place was packed, no matter the time of day, and boy were they happy to see us. But the best deliveries hands-down? The strip clubs! Walking into a strip club as a sixteen-year-old boy, unloading half a dozen kegs into a basement, and then saddling up to the bar while the manager reviewed the invoice and cut a check was the stuff of teenage fantasies. The naked bartenders didn't even ask my age before cracking open a cold beer for my driver and me. The girls working the poles often stopped what they were doing to saunter over for a chat. They knew we were at their level, just there to earn a living, and treated us like colleagues rather than customers (who were not as pleased at the attention we received). I felt like a king each time I walked out of a strip club. Maybe that's why I never felt nervous (or even tempted) to enter one as a customer.

CALL TO ACTION

Master yourself. Moderate your wants. Move with purpose.

12

FAX MACHINES AND TYPEWRITERS

THE ART OF THE WAIT

"First say to yourself what you would be; and then do what you have to do."

—Epictetus

C'*mon. Really?* I'm afraid so. Not quite as much with a fax machine, but sending a typewritten message was (and still is) always worth of the wait for a response. If done well, it can create virtually orgasmic results! From my own romantic experiences, the person receiving a typewritten note from Murph was left gushing way more than a dozen roses had ever induced. The reason is simple. People who care about us feel more appreciated and cared for when we take the time and effort required to create something so personal. In my experience, the idea of a personal touch can even lead to a more literal personal touch. Effort equals intimacy! Funny how that works out.

I was not a Don Juan, Rico Suave, or Cassanova by any stretch of the imagination, so not all of my letters were aimed at getting laid. I remember typing up a letter to the Tampa Ray Rowdies (a professional soccer team from the defunct NASL league). Besides writing how much I loved the colors of their uniforms, I had the balls to write that someday I would don the jersey and play for them. Their response? A typed return letter thanking me for my interest and an autographed trading card from EVERY team member. I was freakin' stoked!

Believe it or not, both of these obscure, archaic mechanisms of communication still exist. For readers who witnessed the fax machine's heyday, how cool and scary was its introduction at your local library or office? The fax machine had a very distinct ring. It sounded like a regular phone call at first, but that was abruptly followed by a long, distinctive beep. After one or two shorter beeps, there was a trademark buzz and whining sound, followed by long pause. Only then came the sound paper being printed and spit out of the machine. Slow as shit. Patience was required. But it was also magical. Information either typed or hand-written from someone on the other side of planet Earth could send us easy-to-read content immediately and directly. No inbox. No scrolling. No algorithm. Just instant, direct messages. I saw some crazy fax receivables in my career–private messages sent by attorneys and movie stars to princes or celebrities. I even read a few anxiety-ridden messages about opening box office numbers (those were the most stressful). Many in the business and entertainment sectors still rely on fax machines (hint: your government), which proves that it still holds value as a secure method of information exchange. Stoics recognized this and often offered perspective on what the meager fax machine really means to the world: security, reliability, and legal validity. Just don't forget to place your fax facedown. It can save you from a lot of embarrassment.

Now for the real treasure – the typewriter. Typewriting, like Stoicism, demands clarity of purpose, discipline, and focused action. You must know what you want to express before you begin, then let your fingers follow with a steady, deliberate movement. There is no backspace or safety net. No editing or second guessing. Just commitment. And when you type something for someone you love, every word feels permanent. There's no delete key for your heart.

Every time I enter a thrift store or see a garage sale, my eyes scan corners for a typewriter. Usually, I'll find one sitting on the ground inside a suitcase-style carrier (the uglier the better). If you believe that the authentic self is the soul made visible, then these ugly suitcases contain the keys to our souls. They are an outlet of authenticity borne of careful planning and deliberate execution of thoughts, expressions and ideas. This is why a typed letter is worth so much more than a superficial gift. The art of typewriting forces you to think far ahead to plot the structure of your words, before planning each detail and embellishment of those words. Only then can you pull a beginning from your brain to mark the paper. Typing forces courage. Ding. Return.

Curiously, I have only one typewriter (practicing moderation). What's funny is its purpose. The machine's current job is to constantly stare at me and plead with me to use it. It's like a dog that stares at its owner, waiting to be taken for a walk or to play fetch. It is my instigator of intent. A spearhead of the taunt. The mission is clear. Choose words with care, then align those words with values. Maybe I'm overthinking this, but as a writer, the typewriter is comparable to a bible for a priest, the canvas to an artist, or the vibrator to an OnlyFans model. It is simultaneously a tool, an inspiration, and a symbol of purpose.

The typewriter, like life, should be a tool of honesty. Its pages command writers to stop hiding and say what they mean. Whether or not you care enough to experience the intimacy of a typewriter, we can all learn a lot from its keys: Make your life count by living it intentionally. Sometimes the way you communicate is itself the message. It's worth the time it takes to consider what sort of message our life choices are sending. Is your message correctly typed, formatted, and edited? Do you send poems with only a handful of meaningful words on each line? Are you double spaced? Double returned? The page is yours. Fill it wisely.

In a world of screen-mediated, easily edited communication, the personal touch of the typewriter has become rare. As a result, it is also more impactful. It's easy to silently fire off dozens of text messages in a few minutes, but the hum and snap from the keys of a typewriter are the music of substance. Texting carries no weight. No presence. No permanence. No real connection. Yet, when someone sits down and types with intention, magic happens. It's like opening Pandora's Box of intention and challenge. That's what Epictetus means in the quote above this chapter: Decide what you want to be, then do what you have to do. Even if it takes longer to plan. Even if you have to wait for results. Think it through and then stay the path.

CALL TO ACTION

Reconnect the right way. Write to someone who thinks they've been forgotten. Make someone feel seen. Start today. Write one real letter this month—typed, handwritten, whatever. The effort is the message.

13

UNLOCKING VICTORY

ONE QUARTER AT A TIME

"It is not that we have a short time to live, but that we waste a lot of it."

—Seneca

In middle school, one of my rich friends told me he was going to bail from school the next morning to go to the Great Adventure amusement park in New Jersey. I was fucking amped when he asked me to go. *Hell yes!* For some unexplained reason (not my grades–maybe they felt sorry for my teacher), my parents actually said yes. When the guy's dad picked us up in a cherry red convertible Corvette, I felt like I was entering a scene from "Ferris Bueller's Day Off." Man, the power and juice that man exuded was impressive. *Classic!*

Since it was a weekday, the park wasn't overcrowded with families, and it felt like anything was possible. Instead of being stuck in a classroom, dropping my pencil every couple of minutes to avoid being called on to answer a question, our crew of truants pulled up to Great Adventure in a luxury automobile with wind-blown hair, psyched for the most epic day ever! We felt like kings walking into a day unexpected fun while everyone else was in school. It was a whole new level of freedom for me. We headed straight to the first ride we saw, the Ferris Wheel, and hopped on. We spent the first few loops planning our ride strategy for the day as we viewed the park from above. Then, midway through the ride, the rain started. *Damn.* At first it was just a drizzle, and we decided that when we got off the Ferris Wheel, we could duck off for a hot dog while we waited for the rain to pass. Then, something dramatically changed. Fighting a sudden desire to shit in my pants as I dangled 300 feet above the earth, I watched (and felt) a black-clouded-fuck-it's-about-to-pour wall of malevolent thunderstorm advance. Before we could even process the sudden change, the heavens opened. Luckily, we were at least covered by our now violently swinging Ferris wheel canopy, which allowed us to watch everyone else in the park run for their lives. Most headed to the exit, probably deciding it was a sign from God to call it a day. We didn't have that choice. The Ferris wheel stopped, and we were stuck dead center at the top. Cloud level. As I began to wonder what it felt like to get struck by lightning or plunge to my death, I also registered a fierce disappointment that the exit was probably our next destination as well. Moments later, the ride's operator hit the go button and our still-swaying gondola slowly cruised to the concrete. Then, a funny thing happened. As the ride worker opened the latch to let us off the ride, the rain suddenly stopped! We were stunned silent for a good few seconds as the sun slowly crept back out. *Yes!* My friend's dad acted like nothing even happened and told us to go have fun. So, that's exactly what we did! We ran wild through that park with a whole new appreciation for our newfound freedom. All alone. Gen X, baby!

After riding all the rides multiple times with no lines, we decided to try something different. Up ahead was the arcade. It was large and… well, glorious. This was my Taj Mahal. A true wonder of the world. How could a building of that size house so many video games? As we entered, the arcade looked even more insanely huge because it was practically empty. A ghost town. When it was crowded, it felt like the San Quentin prison yard at lunchtime. Enjoy, but keep your head on a swivel. Too many toughs at one game? Split. Too many quarters on the screen? Scram. We had none of this. We had the place all to ourselves. Or did we?

We'd been in there for over an hour and were on the verge of running out of quarters. I noticed I was playing each video game with a bit less luster, no longer caring about high scores, when I decided to take a break and walk around the arcade for a bit. I figured we only had a couple more minutes anyway until it was time to leave. I wanted to take it all in and make sure I had played everything I wanted to try. I turned the corner of a long alley and noticed two people. One was a punk groupie—a Nancy Spungen look-alike—and the other was... *What. The. Fuck. It couldn't be. No fucking way...*

At around that age, music was quickly becoming my vice, my identity, my whole existence. I purposely tried to plant songs into my head each day in a certain order to create cool soundtracks for my daily life. I was actively striving for a part-jock, part-punk, part-normal, part-wiseass kind of lifestyle with musical accompaniment. I watched for the right moments to bring each of these personalities out, and music would sometimes dictate which character got to shine. Certain bands had already made a deep impression on me, and one of them was a punk outfit from Queens called the Ramones. There was no doubt it was him. He looked like he had just walked out of the poster on my bedroom wall… the gentle giant: Joey fucking Ramone. Wearing jeans and a leather jacket, he towered over me. I don't know why I needed confirmation, but I asked the punk girl with him, "Is that Joey Ramone?" Without missing a snap of her bubble gum, and with a thick New York attitude, she replied, "Yeah." As I walked past them in awe, Joey *(Joey FUCKING Ramone!)* suddenly turned to me and said, "Hey, kid, how do you play this game?" I turned around to make sure he was talking to me (duh), and then I zeroed in on the game he couldn't figure out—*Journey*. Damn. This was not some time warp, medieval game. Nope. This stupid game was literally about the band called *Journey*. It was a horribly produced video game that looked like shit but thank God I knew how to play it.

After an awkward pause, Joey Ramone looked at me like, "Well?" and we were off. The details of my "teaching" are a blur, but I so remember the weird bonding feeling I had. The dreamlike experience began as we started the game's joint mission. The sense of irony burned a hole in my mind. This game was a gimmick… did Joey think the same about the video game's featured band? He must've. Once the screen faded up from black, and the voiceover announced, "Welcome to Journey. Your mission is to help

Journey retrieve their instruments from the dangers of the five galaxies," Joey shot me a quick, *what-the-hell-is-this?* sort of look.

"Yeah, I know, it's a weird game," I said anxiously. As Joey Ramone and I "Journeyed" though Neil Schon's swim in a river with his guitar, to bouncing off drum kits in outer space, we both knew the game was a shitty, poorly produced, rip-off of Donkey Kong. Or maybe Frogger. The final stage of the game was even more abhorrent: Steve Perry had to avoid the swinging gates to grab his mic stand. I felt bad for all three of us (Joey, most importantly), and I knew my time with the king of punk was drawing to an end. Although I explained each level clearly, let's just say that Mr. Ramone did not get the high score.

"Thanks, kid," was all he said before the gentle giant and his friend wandered off leaving me frozen, reeling it all in. After at least a few minutes, I finally snapped out of it and ran to find my friend. He was not going to believe this! By the time I found my buddy, Joey was already gone. We searched the arcade for him, but he was nowhere in sight. I'm still not sure if my friend ever really believed me.

Whether he believed me or not, I learned a lot from that adventure. First, I know not to just "call it a day" every time it rains. Adapting through setbacks can lead to unexpected rewards. And two, never underestimate the power of small skills and accomplishments. Try new things, learn new skills, and leap outside your comfort zone. Who knows when the unique knowledge of a rare skillset will lead you to a bonding experience with Joey fucking Ramone while hunting down Steve Perry's virtual mic stand! Finally, even in the rush of the greatest and most epic experiences of life, pause a second to take it all in. Fully absorbing a moment in time can lead to beneficial observations.

CALL TO ACTION

Game over? Try again. When you have a bad day or things don't turn out as planned, use that as an opportunity to hunker down and wait out the storm rather than quitting. Take in the details of the moment using all five senses. Notice anything new?

14

A DRINK

PART TWO

"To appreciate the beauty of a snowflake it is necessary to stand out in the cold."

—Aristotle

As I write this, I'm in the early stages of a 100-day reset… not a challenge or "going hard," but an authentic, non-gimmicky reset. I've given the Dry January/Sober October/Lenten Abstinence missions a shot, and sometimes they temporarily worked, but sometimes not. It's an interesting marketing ploy by whoever began the group-project-sobriety trend. I feel like the falseness of creating such a personal change within a public forum is my main reason for inconsistency. To me, it's the same as peddling sobriety the way Hallmark creates (or exaggerates) holidays, by fostering fear and insecurities: If you don't buy that card, or those chocolates, or these flowers, you are a fucking loser. Who even came up with Valentine's Day or Mother's Day, or my most dreaded Father's Day (still waiting for that gift, boys)? Why not just tell people how much you love them whenever you feel it? Why not treat every day like V-Day? Each day should be a time to listen to your gut, your heart, or (in my case) your liver. Special occasions, fads, or forced self-help groups shouldn't be the only time to try something new. I adopted this philosophy back in my twenties, when I finally got up the gumption to enter Hollywood Blvd.

Every day I passed by this bar and, for about a year, it intimidated the shit out of me. Nondescript. Brick façade with a black door that had seen better days. Not at all inviting, yet right near the corner of the busiest spot in touristy Hollywood. This area, although laden with sidewalk stars and wax museums, was not for the meek. At night, especially back in the mid 90's, this establishment was not a place nice people hung around. Just like when we were kids, by the time the streetlights came on, the tourists fled and the vibe dissolved into a Monet of freaks, gang members, homeless folks, drunks, and serial killers. It was a perfect backdrop, I naturally thought, for an average guy in my mid-twenties. The fact that I was spiritually lost and utterly confused by the general direction of my life only added to my reckless desire to enter. One day, on the way home from work, I impulsively decided to go in. Instead of milling about in the ice-cold pool of indecision and doubt, I parked my car in the tiny lot next door and dove in headfirst (is that why they're called dive bars?). First impression: there's a profound difference between a neighborhood bar and a dive bar. When entering a dive, the quickest thing you should do is adjust your eyes and assess the room. With basically no lights on, you've got to acclimate quickly. After that, it's best to walk straight to a seat like you've been there before. Dives like this have mostly bar seating, but Hollywood Blvd did offer some tiny tables with a chair or two against a windowless wall. Bar experts (like me) can tell with a glance when the bartender is a seasoned, salty, one-man show. This guy obviously was, and there was no fucking way he was walking all the way from the bar to attend to my—or anyone's—fancy table needs. To the bar, then. Next, you'd better determine where the regulars sit, because you do not want to poach a barstool in a place like this. Luckily, in my case, it looked like most of the barflies and drunks had already hunkered down in their usual corner spots for the evening. This created nice bookends to a wide-open center spot to plant my ass. Just in case, I watched the bartender closely as I pulled out the seat for any changes in facial expression or body language to indicate I should choose somewhere else to sit. Nothing. *Sweet.* I was in a beer (Budweiser) and a shot (Jameson) phase, so I ordered the Murph special and tipped the bartender five bucks right off the bat. Although I initially sensed apprehension and distrust from the guy, this move seemed to lighten him up. A bit, anyway. It's good advice to *always* tip well on the first round. It sets a tone and diffuses tension. No matter which bar you are in, a well-tipped bartender will look out for you.

As a rule, I like to sip my shots and take pulls from my beer bottle. I usually plan to stay for a while, and there is never a need to go all frat boy with drinks. Besides, that screams *amateur hour* when it comes to imbibing in a dive. So, all settled in with time to kill, I was taking in the moment when the door of the bar opened again. It was a couple of tourists who immediately turned around and left, probably afraid to enter. To prove that I belonged there, and to quell my barely stifled anxiety, I gave the proverbial nod across the bar and received my second round quickly. Same order. It was only then I had the balls to look around some. To my dismay, I hadn't even noticed the very successful English rock star (no, I will not rat him out) passed out at the end of the bar. *Typical Hollywood.*

After another round and some small talk with the bartender, I figured I should get out of there while things were still peaceful. I was in full drifting mode planning to spend the rest of my evening at home listening to Pearl Jam, and maybe even writing the next brilliant novel, when the front door swung open, followed by the sound of a barstool dragging the floor. Someone sat down directly to my left and, out of the corner of my eye, I saw him drop a pair of fine white gloves onto the bar. The bartender didn't say a word as he dropped a beer and a shot in front of him. My kind of guy. No verbal greeting. Silence. As I summoned the courage to turn and give him a nod, he interjected, "How's it going, man?" My elation at having a new friend changed to shock, then a bit of a cringe, as I faced him. On the stool next to me, dressed in a full tuxedo with a completely white face of makeup, sat a fucking mime. Talking. Out loud. *Again, Hollywood.* As the shock wore off, I thought *what the hell,* and settled in to see what this was all about. After some initial chit-chat, he told me he comes in here every day at this time for his fifteen-minute break from the boulevard crowds. This particular evening, he was especially riled up because the tourists weren't tipping much, and a snot nosed kid apparently just kicked him in the balls while the parents stood there and watched. I bought the guy a second round both out of pity, and because I couldn't believe I was drinking with a mime. He slammed the second round systematically, slid the gloves back on, and told me he was back "on the clock," before disappearing back into the frenzy like a beleaguered vet. *Surreal.*

While contemplating my recent interaction, the English rocker woke up and was promptly "escorted" out of a back door by a very large "friend." Evidently, the escort had been lurking out of sight in a dark corner of the room all evening. Never saw him. Since all good things must come to an end, I bid farewell to the bartender and nodded to a few others before departing the way of the mime. No one batted an eye or said a word as I left—they still had work to do. Yet something changed as I walked outside and breathed in the smoggy evening air: I held my head a little higher. In fact, for just a moment, I wondered if this is what soldiers felt like after storming the beaches of Normandy and living to tell the tale. Ten steps later, however, I realized my car had been towed. *Fuck. Hollywood.*

Several years later, after moving out of the area, I was passing through and decided to drop by the old place. Inside, it smelled sanitized. There was a new, more modern layout and plenty of seating–maybe even a dance floor. It was a lot brighter, but the bartender was a total prick. Some things just don't last. That's why we should try hard to live in the moment and take advantage of opportunities as life presents them, even if it makes us feel nervous or unprepared. Similarly, things often work out when we make a point to indulge our curiosities and confront our fears with acceptance of the unknown, with respect for others, and with kind intentions. Remember that time is nothing more than a collection of single moments. How you color or confirm those moments is independently and emphatically yours. Seize these moments! Own them. When the idea of a new adventure makes you anxious, smile and believe in yourself. Just remember to look at the parking signs before entering. Your mind is an expensive thing to get towed.

CALL TO ACTION

Hesitation and delay are thieves of life. Enter now, while the moment is yours. Take the plunge. Take a risk. Take a leap straight into the unknown. But most importantly, take the opportunities life gives you to journey outside your comfort zone. Face your fear and dive!

15

THE WORLD MAY BE CHANGING

BUT MUSIC STILL MATTERS

"He who lives in harmony with himself lives in harmony with the universe.

—Marcus Aurelius

As a latchkey kid, I had a lot of time on my hands. With two brothers fighting over limited TV channels, I ended up spending a lot of time in my room looking at posters, staring up at the ceiling, and listening to music. Those hours alone in my room didn't feel lonely at the time, but looking back I realize that music was filling a space I didn't have words for. When you're a kid trying to figure out who you are, a great song can feel like someone out there already understands you.

My parents had a small record collection, but they were not super into music, so they didn't have a variety of genres to choose from. For me, exploring a wide variety of music genres felt like an escape from the confines of expectations and into the diverse worlds of others. I felt (and still do feel) liberated when I dig for records that are not found in the front section of a shop. The wide variety of music out there is like a vast library offering countless opportunities for creative expression and inspiration. I just want to explore further and further away from the norms of my existence and into the minds of these artists. It's hard to explain the depth of my musical passion.

This is why I began to love our family trips into NYC as a kid. Not so much to experience the city, although I thought that part was nuts and wildly entertaining at the same time. Back then, the mentally insane–not the cliché' phrase, the literally insane–practically owned every corner of the neighborhoods near the burned-out buildings and apocalyptic backdrop of the city. The locals never even seemed to notice them anymore. They were everywhere engaging in controlled chaos (like reading from a non-existent bible), more distracting displays (like screaming into audio/PA equipment), or the super aggressive people who launched themselves at random strangers in angry tirades or desperate frenzies. These poor people held court for anyone who would listen. Gazing out from the back seat of the family Dodge Dart was like an ever-changing front row seat to a free theater of life.

When I was in the eighth grade, I scored a cheap record player from my aunt's garage and had nothing to play besides my parents' John Denver and Elvis records. That wasn't cutting it. I wanted to listen to music that no one else had, so I saved enough money to purchase my first record. With some major persuasion, my parents drove us into the city for a trip to Bleeker Bob's record shop in Greenwich Village.

Don't get me started on the Village. My dad worked in the midtown area with high-rises and business suits. In comparison, the Village was crazy and diverse. More burned-out buildings, freaks everywhere, Tompkins Square Park, and people from all walks of life. I remember seeing a sign on the sidewalk that just said "free sex" with arrows pointing towards an open door with a staircase. *Outstanding* (and no, I never got the chance to see if that was a real deal or not).

In retrospect, walking into Bleeker Bob's with my family was hilarious and absurd. We had absolutely no business being there, nor did I know what the heck I was going to buy. But I had my paper route money and my parents' attention was waning, so as my family nervously loitered, I went straight to the punk rock section. It just drew me in. The artwork of the album covers in that genre called to me. Back then, MTV was actually a music channel, but it also aired low-end documentaries from time to time. One showcased the punk rock scene of Southern California including a live concert from the Hollywood Palladium. One of the bands from the show was not from SoCal but the UK. I flipped through the record display and there it was… Charged GBH'S *City Baby Attacked by Rats*, LP. The cover had a kid in some type of juvenile bondage outfit, and he was playing with blocks that spelled out the record title. A bunch of rats were surrounding him, bloodied and ready to pounce. It was an animated concept and oddly attractive to look at. I decided that this would be my first record!

Checking the price, I figured I still had enough cash to buy one more, so I hit the new wave section. *Whamo!* Found my second record … The Smith's *The Queen is Dead*! I was so pumped when I got to the checkout counter with my selections. My parents were horrified by my choices but just shook their heads and let me check out. The punk rock girl with a Mohawk who was working the register, though, gave me a nonchalant appreciative nod and even threw in a Bleecker Bob's sticker as confirmation of her approval. I felt so cool, and the naivety of youth allowed me to think I was now a full-fledged NYC member of the punk scene. Take that, Strong Island!

In reality, I had no clue. I paid for the records, and my family quickly rushed to the car and back to the comparatively sterile suburbs of the Island. But that visit hooked me into music, despite my age, and I eagerly anticipated my next trip to NYC. My brothers made fun of me the entire way home, and my parents remained silent. I couldn't have cared less as I stared at the two record covers, inhaled the smell of fresh vinyl, and studied every detail. I spent the rest of that day and night in my room, door closed, blasting the records over and over. Life was perfect. It may sound dramatic, but that moment in the record store felt like claiming a piece of independence. A piece of myself. The records weren't just music to me—they were proof that I could choose something to be uniquely mine. Not what my school expected, not what my parents listened to, just something that spoke to me alone.

As my musical tastes progressed through vinyl and cassette tapes, it was time to level up as a true music connoisseur–live concerts. Not sure how I pulled it off, but my parents let me attend my first show alone. I was still in junior high and cell phones were not yet a thing, so Mom and Dad basically had to drop my friend and me off in a vast parking lot, offer us a quick "Be careful," and then bolt. I'm sure it was stressful for them, but I was in heaven. We saw The Cure with 10,000 Maniacs as the opening act at Jones Beach Theater on Long Island. What a venue to see my first show! I love the beach, and to this day am probably the biggest surfing fan alive who doesn't actually surf (*King of the Kooks*). As my mom drove away, I could feel the salty ocean air pushing across the parking lot and into the amphitheater. I stood there breathing it all in until the car was out of sight. It was time to complete the pre-show mission–finding someone to buy us alcoholic drinks. We saw a few girls we knew on our way inside. Of course, they knew my modus operandi and quickly rushed over with a handful of cash. They had the same intention as us. I collected the girls' money (including a little extra to cover my services as beverage coordinator) and headed straight for the bar.

Keep in mind, again, that I was only in eighth grade when I approached the huge stranger wearing a leather jacket, studs, nose piercings and multi-colored hair with my usual business proposition. He looked like someone who was either totally willing to help out or would thoroughly kick my ass. This was the deal I proposed, "I need six Bartle and James wine coolers (flavor does not matter) and I'll give you enough cash to pay for your next two beers as well. Deal?" *Score!* We collected our fruity bottles and stood in the corner together slamming them down before the cops or security caught us with them. We mesmerized the girls, and they wanted to hang out with us for a short time. After the first round, and this time with much more confidence, I found another contributor to our delinquency (same type) who helped with our next alcoholic transaction. After that, it was time for the show to begin, so we dumped the drinks into large soda cups and headed for our seats. The girls had seats near us, and we watched the sun set together while a then 18-year-old Natalie Merchant drank and poured beer over her head while snapping a bull whip.

Darkness approached, and the ocean fog rolled in right on cue. The stage lights dropped, and The Cure walked onstage. *Holy shit.* What a show! They were unreal. When the show ended, we exited the amphitheater with thousands of people, and still buzzing from the drinks and the music, we looked for my friend's mom. As cars cleared the parking lot, we finally found her and climbed in. I rolled down the window and took a final breath of that salty sea air knowing full well that my life had just changed. A path of life had unlocked that I was determined to travel from that moment on. Live music, baby! The feeling has never left me.

Fast forward through many years and hundreds of shows, and I still treasure the memory of every single one. I've seen all types from CBGB Sunday matinees to the Felt Forum in NYC. I've been to Bridge School and multiple other festivals, all 45 Pearl Jam shows (yes, all—and counting), and legendary French Quarter pop ups. It never ceases to amaze me and never gets old—the atmosphere surrounding the shows. I soak it in like a life force. The parking lots, the bathroom lines, even the option (back then) to buy tickets from the back of a Sears or JC Penney. Can you imagine? It's hard enough now to find a salesperson from one of those places just to buy some lame pants and a shitty tie for work. Back then, there what a whole secondary counter in the back of the store (fully staffed) that only sold concert tickets. It was beautiful. The best part were the ticket prices, which were actually affordable. From a musical perspective, Gen X was so lucky.

Shows back then brought fans a sense of belonging. We experienced it all together: the anticipation, the unity, and the openness to meeting others, partying, and just enjoying life for the next few hours. We were completely immersed in the moment. That was it. People were so amped to be tighter… .a part of the vibe. Just to reiterate, there were no phones back then. We all went to a show and watched the musicians on stage (or people making out in the row in front of us). Our focus and attention to the band were on point, because there was nothing else to do. No distractions. We were there for the music. Bands thrived on this, and so did the crowds. *Pure bliss.*

Marcus Aurelius talked about living in harmony with yourself. For me, music has always been the fastest path there. When a song hits you the right way, it quiets the noise in your head. That's harmony—not perfection. Just an alignment between your mind, your memory, and the moment you're standing in.

Full disclosure, my memory of things, academically speaking, is sometimes unreliable, and I always found schoolwork difficult. Memorization was challenging for me, and some subjects were almost impossible to learn or retain. However, when a certain song comes on by a band that I've seen live, I can pinpoint every detail of when I saw them, what I was wearing, who I was with, and what I experienced. I remember the sights, sounds, smells, tastes and feelings of the experience with flawless detail. That, my friends, is a pure love, respect, and obsession with music which transcends academic ability and MUST always be a part of my life. Music cures all. I strongly recommend that you intentionally highlight music as an important part of your life. The experience of music is rarely regretted.

CALL TO ACTION

Turn up the songs that defined you. Go see a band live. Let yourself get lost in the sound for a couple of hours without distraction. Sometimes the fastest way back to yourself is through a song you forgot you loved.

16

TRAVEL SOCCER

AND THE PHENOMENON KNOWN AS HOUSING

"He who has a why to live for can bear almost any how."

—Friedrich Nietzsche

I'm late to the game. Stoic philosophy and the orbital advantages it provides came to me somewhat late in life. Had I followed Stoicism in my younger days, I may have viewed these housing opportunities not as anxiety driven, faux stepfamily encounters, but instead with the notion that what I do not know, is what I know. I had a lot to learn, and regarding the concept of "Housing" during the travel soccer season, I guess my parents learned a lot too.

One of the many sacrifices modern parents must make involves children's sports and how much time (and money) they are willing to invest in them. These decisions are always tough for parents, especially as they watch travel teams destroy what was once a coveted recreational pastime. Gen X grew up with solid recreational teams and leagues, and if you were good enough to be "selected," travel teams were the path of progression. A commitment to travel ball meant that every weekend in the summer, Memorial Day, 4th of July, you name it–instead of relaxing, you were forced to drive (sometimes through multiple states) to play in tournaments. My travel sport was soccer. Kudos to my parents who never (or at least not to me) professed anger or resentment about these adventures. They never said no to my dreams, often sacrificing their own personal plans to let me play. At the time, I took it completely for granted. I now realize the sincere dedication they showed, and I make every effort to pass that along to my own family.

Now that appropriate gratitude has officially been given, I should now mention a serious glitch in the Gen X travel ball system. Housing. There's no way this could ever exist in today's legal environment, but my soccer team and

I defined it as follows: On game weekends, our team traveled to tournaments on Friday mornings. We played one game Friday evening, then we met a local team with kids of similar ages and genders. After brief greetings, our parents handed us off. It's exactly the way you are picturing it. The families of the opposing teams literally "hosted" the kids from our team for the entire weekend. No parents. Complete strangers. Competitive environment. Great idea. Picture your parents driving across state lines, not knowing anyone, saying "hello, nice to meet you," to a random family standing in a hotel parking lot or on a soccer field, and then just tossing you a sleeping bag and driving away. I remember watching my parents' car pull away more than once feeling a strange mix of excitement and dread. Part of me thought it was awesome—total freedom for the weekend. The other part wondered what the hell I had just been dropped into. I never said that out loud as a kid, though. I just slung the sleeping bag over my shoulder and tried to pretend I belonged there. So weird.

After each game, the host family would either hang out all day by the fields (torture) or go back home (potential torture). Sometimes they would treat us to lunch (heaven) or even worse, take us to a G-rated movie. First problem: When the first game of a tournament was AGAINST the host team, especially considering that the games were often very intense and scrappy, sometimes even the parents would get into it. Very awkward. I remember one instance in South Jersey when there was a brawl between parents and coaches after the game. Once the situation was (somewhat) resolved, my team had to go home with the enemies, I mean, hosts. My coach was shaking his head when we left, but we had nowhere else to sleep. What else could we do?

Second problem: We didn't get to choose which family was going to serve as our guardian for the weekend, and every time I sat in the back of their car driving to their house, I assessed the neighborhoods and prayed I would get a nice (or at least safe) one. Some were. Some definitely were not. I always tried to keep a poker face. That's the part no one talked about. When you're thirteen years old and sleeping in a stranger's house, you're constantly reading the room—trying to figure out the rules, the personalities, the landmines. It was like a crash course in adapting to people you didn't understand yet. Stoics talk about accepting circumstances you can't control. Travel soccer housing was basically a weekend seminar in that philosophy—whether we realized it or not.

Some of my less respectful teammates, however, were bad about opening their mouths to "critique" the house while pulling into the driveway. Super awkward. I'll admit that one time, I purposely pissed in the family's shower because I didn't get any breakfast. Another time, my teammate fist-fought the host player nightly. The worst was when there were no extra beds in the house and we had to sleep on the floor. As a kid, I didn't realize how risky the whole situation was. As an adult, I am shocked that no liability forms were signed, that no one ended up in a hospital (or worse), and that no one ever filed a lawsuit (that I know of).

I am still amazed by the audacity and trust levels of the adults who let this happen. It was a ritual that clearly violated common-sense child endangerment policies. Yet there are some kids I met on those trips that I still remember well and wonder about. When it was our turn to host, my parents were very chill. They understood the assignment. The toughest hosting experience was when our family was assigned the loudest, cockiest kids in the league who were well-known for their lack of manners. That sucked. My family just rolled our eyes, stayed cordial, and counted down the minutes until they left.

Third problem: When it came to the actual soccer tournaments, my team almost always made it to the finals on Sunday afternoons. This put a burden on the host families, who always managed to express their disgust. When we hosted, the eliminated teams typically played badly and departed late Saturday to beat the traffic and salvage the rest of the weekend. Only once, we hosted some guys from a seriously talented team who won the whole tournament. That felt great, because they were very thankful to my parents. Imagine the anxiety, though, if kids and their parents were forced into this process today? How would they interact? Would they just ask for chargers and stare at their screens to avoid talking? Knowing we had to house these players right after a game seems crazy now, but in terms of learning to behave professionally and to embrace occasional discomfort, something like this could really help people chill out a little and learn to roll with the punches. Modern travel ball players could use a bit of perspective as a reminder that ball is just a game. The real challenge of life is to show a kind spirit and gracious hospitality, even when you feel uncomfortable.

Side note: cleaning out my closet the other day, I found a small box filled with patches. Dozens and dozens of soccer patches from teams around the world that I played against. We used to exchange these at tournaments.

They're all really cool. Holding those patches again re-minded me that soccer weekends weren't just chaos. They were connection. Kids from different towns, different families, different lives—meeting for ninety minutes on a field and then going back to their worlds. At the time it felt so normal, but looking back it feels pretty special. Different logos, different styles. After each game, we lined up to shake hands and exchange patches with kids from opposing teams. Of course, if your patch sucked, someone was bound to say something, which usually caused some pushing, shoving, or shit talking. With any luck, the shit talkers didn't have the crappy patch kids as a host. If they did, that's always a tough life lesson. Other than that, though, it was an awesome memory.

I tried to focus on the positive aspects of the housing experience. I really did. When all else failed (or I complained vigorously with my parents after the first night) a bug-infested motel room in rural Pennsylvania would become my home for the weekend. Yes, there were stares from the host family, but we pulled out the old "I'm not feeling well" excuse if we had to. When God was in a particularly comical mood, we had to play our host team in the finals. This only happened once, but to make matters worse, we won the tournament with a last-second goal in a very chippy, contentious match. Talk about awkward. Thankfully, our families felt the storm coming and grabbed our sleeping bags and gear prior to the start of the game. My coach, the team, and all the parents had never left a parking lot so quickly as we did that day with our trophy and first place medals.

CALL TO ACTION

90% of parenting is just being there. Today, show up for someone in your life the way someone once showed up for you.

17

BE YOUR OWN MENTOR

BE YOUR OWN LIGHT

"Don't put your purpose in someone else's hands– hold it always in your own."

—Epictetus

My favorite type of mentor is no-nonsense and blunt with the truth. The biggest mistake of my life was ignoring the mentors that were right in front of me—like the teacher who stayed after class to offer advice I barely heard, or the Director who tried to teach me patience and a sense for business. Arrogance. That's OK though, because thankfully I am much wiser now, and guess what? Since my ignorance didn't kill me, I am now able to teach others the lessons from my mistakes. Lead by example. Be authentic. Attitude of gratitude. Keep smiling. Keep trying. Service above self. The more you give, the more you receive. The lessons I've learned the hard way could go on and on. Learn from my mistakes, though, and you will have a hard time finding the negative in life. I guess I've been my own mentor.

The truth is, if I had known I needed a mentor growing up, I would have been more selective. Again, learn from my mistakes. When considering mentorship, take a moment to relax, take a deep breath, and think carefully about what a mentor could bring to your table of life. Who is your idol? Have you met him or her? What is it about this person that attracts your admiration? A mentor is someone you have known or followed for a while who fits the narrative of what you want your life to be. It could be an icon of your professional goals, an artist whose methods speak to your soul, or maybe just a good, kind person with a character you admire. After that, note whether this person tends to give more than they receive and help when needed, or if assistance is given only when it benefits his/her own life. When you are certain of this person's nature and you have made your decision, then ask him or her (if possible) if he/she is willing to offer guidance and support as a mentor. If you don't know your mentor, simply study the characteristics you admire and apply them to your own life.

Unfortunately, it is sometimes difficult to identify needed traits in others when you're already struggling, out of work, battling demons, having trouble with relationships, or otherwise just lost in the sauce. That's when you need a mentor the most. If you don't have one, try to mentor yourself by discovering which (healthy) activities help you to chill out and relax. Stress and anxiety are the enemies of solutions. Learn to relax, and that's when the stage lights will pop back on. Showtime. After that, all you have to do is stay focused on your goals. Too easy, right? It's true. If you believe in your goals hard enough, picture them often enough and with enough detail, you will start to form a path to these goals in your mind–and you will get your shot. It will come to you. But you must be ready. Don't be one of these people in the "hollow talent" category. Those are the folks that have ideas of dreams, but they don't fill them in with the details needed to make the dreams reality. The details are the plan. No plan? No success.

The last office I inhabited in Los Angeles was on a movie studio lot. It was situated perfectly on the second floor of a small, historic building. From my window, I could see who was walking in and walking out of our building. Many of these were A-listers of the entertainment industry. I could hear everything they were saying! When I

first realized this, I was excited. I thought I might gain ex-
pert insight about life in the entertainment industry by
eavesdropping. This rarely happened. What did often happen, and frustrated me to no end, was the periodical arrival
of the "hangers-on," who loitered around the parking lot.
Sometimes they seemed to appear out of nowhere (no idea
how they kept getting onto the lot) to cry and plead with
the ambushed A-lister or Producer for jobs. Don't get me
wrong: I don't fault these people for knowing what they
want and going after it aggressively. It was the way they approached the profession that bothered me (and their more
successful targets). The people who showed up uninvited
to beg for things they hadn't earned were all looking for a
short cut. They weren't asking for a position based on talent or worth. Just whining and entitlement. Man, it pissed
me off. Don't approach the greats of your industry asking
for handouts, when most of them had to climb to where
they are the hard way. Earn your keep or fucking buzz off.
Seneca nailed it: "Luck is what happens when preparation
meets opportunity." Watching through my window, I realized that truly successful people don't wait around for mentors—they create conditions for themselves. That's a lesson
I could have applied much earlier in life.

Another lesson I learned more slowly than I like to admit is that luck plays a part in most success stories. Understand that, and it can save you from a lot of self-loathing. No one is where they are today without some kind of luck playing a role in their journeys. In my youth, I always shunned the luck factor, staunchly believing that it was me, and only me, that will get me to my goals. To live and die by my own sword. Stupid. In fact, we are the engines of our lives, but luck is the jolt that revs it. When luck shows up, don't stubbornly turn off the engine, hit the gas!

While working that same backlot job, I got to regularly see the studio's walking tours. Dozens of tourists followed guides around the lot, learning about the rich history of the buildings or that giant sound stage surrounding the office. Most of the tourists did not give two shits about the history. They were there to see celebrities. Not judging–I get it. I'm a fan, too! My office building happened to be THE major attraction of every tour. As I watched the throng of folks edge closer to my window, I had a comedic advantage. I knew exactly who was at meetings in our office, and who was about to leave or show up. Sometimes there was just a matter of seconds between when an entire group of tourists walked past then looked away and when the biggest movie star stepped outside to catch up with a rock star or rapper.

Occasionally, the tour groups got lucky when a celebrity or athlete pulled up in the studio golf cart for a meeting. The point is, there was usually only a matter of seconds during the transition from out of the building to inside the building, and either people were at the right place at exactly the right time, or not. Luck.

Everyday life is like a Hollywood backlot. Rather than wait for a handout, because you might wait a long time, take the initiative to create the sort of life that could attract the kind of mentor you need. Take the time, do the work, make the effort on your own first, not only for your self-worth, but also as an example for others who may not know how. Oddly, attempting to be your own mentor is a perfect test to determine if you are capable of becoming a mentor to others. It is also a deeply soul-searching adventure. Am I really mentor-worthy? Yes? onward. No? Figure out why not and start working on it. No one else will push you to self-motivate, but the effect (and rewards) generated from helping others can often create motivation more than accolades from A-listers ever could. By mentoring others, we mentor ourselves, so don't seek the shallowness of external approval as your measure of success. Leave that up to the entitled fucks on the Hollywood backlots to fight over. You will pass them on the mountain as they gasp for air. Be content walking in the shadows of success and focusing on helping others along the way. The work you put into service and self-improvement will create luck, attract selfless mentors, and build more meaningful success than you expect. It's all about healthy focus.

CALL TO ACTION

Your self-worth is way more important than the approval of others. Invest wisely in yourself, and you will gain the approval of the those that matter.

18

BLOCK PARTIES AND STREET GAMES
IMAGINATION OF THE POOR

"The happiness of your life depends upon the quality of your thoughts."

—Marcus Aurelius

In most of the places I've lived, especially in NY, there was a comical balance between respect and hatred for our neighbors. Not just the next-door neighbors, but the whole street–or at least our whole block. Sometimes, a dozen houses participated in drama, but things stayed mostly civil. Choosing our battles was an artform of street-wisdom that could affect an entire summer or beyond. Hatred could find solace in patience for a while, until it suddenly flared back up just when we thought the beef was over. As a kid, I didn't fully understand why grown adults carried grudges over things like parking spots, loud music, or who forgot to return a ladder. Back then it seemed ridiculous. It still does, if you ask me. As a grown adult, I realize that adults are just kids with mortgages. Same emotions, same insecurities. The block taught me early that peace isn't something that just appears. Someone has to first decide it's worth protecting. During the short, but refreshing, times of neighborhood peace, some wise sage would inevitably suggest we a block party.

First decision–day and time. Usually this was settled out on the sidewalk (battlefield) by the most alpha moms on the block. For some reason, they always picked a Saturday in July, usually the hottest day of the year, to shut down the streets (sans permits or permissions of any sort). They used a hodgepodge of barricades like trash cans and cars to block traffic. The starting time was early afternoon and usually ran until evening. There were always neighbors who staunchly voted no to the block party but were always overruled. Our neighborhood seemed to thrive on drama, and it was survival of the fittest. Some just couldn't take it, completely disobeyed the "rules of the party," and either left early (wimps), stayed too long (drunks), or didn't bring any food (cheapskates). Since the behavior of these rogues was predictable, it was always considered during the planning phase.

Next decision – the set-up. The location was determined by who brought what, who did most of the planning, and who did most of the work. Certain houses brought out grills, and we all contributed tables. Drinks were on our own. From what I remember, drinking in NY wasn't a big deal. The Budweiser always flowed steadily, but the consumption was usually tame. In the South, forget about it. If you don't walk into a party with your own cooler of drinks (and a spare in the back of your truck), you'll get the southern side-eye and be lucky to receive the next invite. Just facts.

After the initial stress of getting everything started, I liked to pause to look around and just absorb all the sights and smells. These quiet block party pauses were probably my first experiences with intentional gratitude. Not the performative kind people call attention to—just the simple feeling that life, at the exact moment, was enough. Hot asphalt, burgers cooking on a grill, cursing out the Mets, ice cream bomb pops melting down the wrists of kids… For a few minutes, nobody cared about money, status, or problems. We were just there in the moment. Marcus Aurelius would have approved. Hear the laughter and the cursing.

The gossiping and the kids at play. The block parties on Long Island were a glimpse of what an ideal life could be—the real deal. Neighbors relaxing in the middle of a street and, for just a moment in time, enjoying each other in a comforting and stress-free environment. Eventually, though, the drama always started–usually initiated by a single asshole. Except that one year when the dirtbags from the next town over found out about the party and came to crash it. Thankfully the drama usually happened late in the evening, because sometimes fists flew, tables flipped, and the police had to get involved to unravel the streets. It was better to finish eating before all that started.

As for all the maniac kids on our block, this was just another day in life of a concrete jungle childhood. Every day was another adventure for us. Stickball was a combination of handball and a broomstick that we stole from somebody's garage. The moms always found out and got furious, but oh well. It was fun, until we upgraded to tennis racquets. Our strength turned homers into multi-block sprints, and it became too much of a hassle to hop fences and rummage around private property to find the ball. Bike ramps made from anything we found lying around were a risky form of entertainment we enjoyed, but considering the frequency of injury, we didn't build them often. Our favorite game, and hands-down the most exciting (and least costly) street game of them all was KICK THE CAN! All we needed to play was an empty soda or beer can. We threw some rocks inside it, and we were off to the races. We could play with five or twenty players, and the objective was easy. Select someone to be "it," and then he/she had to count ten seconds with closed eyes. Everyone else ran to hide. And wait. And wait. The person who was "it" placed the can in the middle of the street. If he saw someone hiding, he ran over to the can and shouted, "Tap tap, tap, I see Murph in the bushes by Mrs. Munson's house." If that was you, you were out and had to sit on the curb. As more people got caught, the stakes ran higher. The only way to be "freed" was get to the can and kick it while the person who was "it" was distracted or chasing another person. Some of the greatest euphoria and adrenaline rushes in my life came from that game. What I loved the most about it wasn't just the rush. It was the fact that, for a few hours, nobody was the weird kid, the poor kid, the tough kid, or the shy kid. We were just players. You could be the quiet kid who barely spoke all summer and suddenly became the hero who freed everyone with one perfect kick. That kind of redemption sticks with you.

Sometimes during a game, we would have about twenty kids already called out and only one remaining. This was when it got seriously exciting! The "it" person eventually got impatient, or just too cocky for a second, leaving the can unguarded. It happened every time. Out of fucking nowhere, the sole survivor shot like a bullet out of the bushes, from under a car, or behind a tree—sprinting their ass off towards the can. A furious race for the can started, and before the "it" person could tap the can–BLAM! Someone always kicked the can, and then everyone ran. Oh my, did that set off the whole street into a cornucopia of adrenalin rushes and expletives! There was extreme shit-talking and a level of energy usually only comparable (I hear) to someone's first ever hit off a crack pipe. Ineffable! Depending on who was it at the time, the game could be called anytime we felt like being an asshole or a bad sport. I admit it. I pulled this shit myself a couple of times, only to be yelled at by my mom to go back outside. This usually morphed into the same treatment from my friends. Completely justified. Guess what I learned… not to be a pussy about a game.

From a simple game of Kick the Can, wise Stoics may observe a quiet lesson about moving through life. The game

(although quite simple) demands presence of mind, awareness of others around us, and the ability to react quickly
without overreacting. As a child, I was obviously not a
Stoic. I did still value the laughter, the chase, and the unexpected ricochet of the can in a way I couldn't put into words
at the time. Without realizing it, this simple street game
was quietly shaping my character. It taught patience while
hiding under cars or in bushes, courage when sprinting towards the can, humility when caught cheating, and awareness of others. Stoicism in sneaker. Stay alert. Stay calm.
Act when the moment is right.

CALL TO ACTION

Take the lead in your community. Host something simple—a
cookout, a street game, a backyard gathering. You'd be surprised how quickly strangers become neighbors when someone
is brave enough to start the party.

19

PHOTO ALBUMS

AND THE PRESERVATION OF BAD DECISIONS

*"True happiness is to enjoy the present, without anxious depend-
ence upon the future."*

—Seneca

Imagine a world (or better yet, the part of town you live in) with an abandoned mini mall, empty storefronts, and a rundown grocery store barely able to keep the lights on. The parking lot is a wasteland of potholes, trash, empty shopping carts and lost hope. Now imagine a small, shed-like booth, about the size of an expressway toll box, placed right in the middle of that parking lot. It had windows on one side, kind of like a drive thru. In fact, it was a drive thru. But instead of placing food orders to make us fat and feel like shit, we handed them rolls of film. I realize that camera film has made a small resurgence in recent years, but I will explain further for readers who are unfamiliar with the concept. Camera film looked like a C-battery-sized plastic canister with a slightly smaller plastic tube inside. The inside tube held the rolled-up film strip with "negative" images of photos taken on our cameras. These booths existed because, instead of the instant gratification of seeing a picture on a phone right after clicking, we had to hand over the hope of good photos to a complete stranger in a sketchy booth. We entrusted the booth people to "develop" our memories by sticking the film into a various chemicals or machines in the darkness. From this, they created a photograph the size of an index card to be picked up in the drive through. This process could take up to a couple of weeks. The anticipation and trust required for this archaic developing process was intense.

I remember sitting in the car with my mom while she picked up a roll we had dropped off weeks earlier. We tore open the photo envelope right there in the parking lot. Our nerves were next level. That was the strange thing about film—you weren't just developing photos. You were developing memories. Moments of your actual life that you couldn't take back.

The popular shift towards in-store film processing services at local supermarkets and drugstores changed the game, but even then it was an exercise of trust and patience. Would you ever hand over your phone to a stranger to check out your photos? Didn't think so. We did it all the time. Half the time, we waited so long to get our film developed that we couldn't even remember what was on the film. We just dropped it off without making eye contact and prayed there was nothing provocative enough for the employee to steal or duplicate. Given the limited number of possible photos on a single roll of film, and the cost involved to get it developed, most people took pictures carefully and with intention. The slow, deliberate photo shoot requiring observation, contemplation, and prioritization is becoming a lost art. We have replaced the thoughtful process of composition with filters and the ability to take over a hundred crap shots for every one we use. There is no longer a need for skill, precision, or patience.

Waiting for a roll of mystery film to process was both exciting and stressful. We worried about all sorts of things: Was the lighting okay or too dark? Who is even in these pictures? Ex girlfriend? A beloved pet who died last year? I hope the faces are focused this time. Did anyone blink? I know I blinked, I always blink, I hate that. We just had to wait and see. To make it worse, when we didn't like the pictures we picked up, there was no crop feature except a pair of scissors. And we couldn't just delete the ones we didn't like and choose a different one because, most of the time, these images were the only physical memento you would ever have of that day, event, or occasion. Considering you deemed the moment worthy enough for the time and money required to take photos in the first place, the memory was usually important enough to keep even the bad photographs.

Looking through those albums now, I'm amazed by how many bad decisions are now preserved with perfect clarity. They remind me that life wasn't supposed to be edited to perfection. The mistakes were part of the story. We are not doing ourselves any favors by creating an image of digital perfection for life that reality can never reproduce. These unrealistic standards are damaging entire generations of souls.

I guess it's only natural to want your memories to be curated. This is why a lot of Gen X photos from the days of 35mm film the are torn (cropped), marked on (edited), or crumpled up (temporarily moved to the trash file, then later removed to preserve the nostalgia). Old-school photography was a lot like hunting… .we waited for the perfect shot, lined it up carefully, kept a steady hand, breathed out gently, then whammo—hit the click button (trigger). Sometimes we nailed it, sometimes it was a waste of effort. But once we had amassed enough of photos, it was time to pull out the photo albums.

Most of these storied treasures were nothing more than binders with sleeves on the inside to store photos. We could tell when a binder contained photos by the creative designs we drew, painted, or stuck all over the outside cover. A lot of thought went into deciding how to organize the photos. Chronologically or categorically? Seasonally? By friend level? Photo albums made us think clearly and thoughtfully about each moment of life to create the best layout. Photo albums were the social media pages of Gen X, providing a visual show-and-tell for friends and family to review and either enjoy (like) or absolutely rip apart (dislike). We couldn't be lazy when the future perception of events was on the line, so we had to make the display count. Much like Facebook and Instagram, photo albums opened the windows of our lives for others to peek through and either laugh, cry, make fun of us, or accept being made fun of. I remember being downright embarrassed when my boys discovered a tattered photo album of mine while rummaging through a hallway closet. Talk about quick thinking. "Dad, who is that girl? That's not Mom? Dad, you're holding a beer… how old were you?" Watching my kids flip through those pages made me feel both pride and mild terror in equal parts.

There were moments I had completely forgotten—old friends, bad apartments, questionable fashion choices. But there were also moments that reminded me how lucky I'd been. It was funny to realize that the albums didn't just document my life and past. They also quietly documented how much I had changed.

Just as vintage cameras once captured the world in the rich tones of 35mm film, so too should we color our thoughts with light and intention. Take time to consider a moment before pulling out your phone to take a photo. Is the moment worth your time and effort? If not, perhaps it's better to leave it in your pocket and just be present in real time. If the photo is worth the effort, don't forget to also be mindful as you take it all in with all five senses. It's easy to lose track of reality when we constantly view the world through a screen. One more thing, always remember to refuse the negatives as they develop.

CALL TO ACTION

Laugh every single day… even if the joke is on you. Years from now, those imperfect moments may be the ones you're most grateful you captured.

20

LEAVE IT BETTER THAN YOU FOUND IT

"Train yourself to strive for giving, rather than receiving."

—Gaius Musonius Rufus

I don't know why I'm wired like this, but when I see someone who is complacent, low energy, or with a poor work ethic, it bugs the shit out of me. I couldn't care less about the corner office, expense account, annual awards, or other corporate trappings people chase like a religion; if others are doing most of your work, then you will receive zero respect from me. I value working with people who will bust their asses for the good of the world. A work ethic in service to something real. Showing up to a volunteer event or site is like walking into an ideal world. The energy that fills the air shifts when everyone is there for the greater good.

This always gets me wondering about my own place in the scheme of life. Will anything I create or do stand the test of time? Are there any Gen X artifacts that still exist anymore? And by "exist," I mean do they still hold value or relevance to the everyday lives of younger people? I guess microwave ovens are still around. Post-it notes are thriving. Vinyl records are at least accessible, although you may have to crate-dive for the good ones! Camcorders, VHS tapes, and pay phones are obsolete. Cable TV began in our era and has grown into a monster, whether for good or bad. Video arcades are kind of back in business, but most are marketed to adults now. Do I even care? What is it with Gen Xers that compel us to hold on to the items and icons of our youth for dear life? Are we still angst-filled? Raging against a machine that no longer exists? Or worse, a machine that has morphed into our wildest, most horrible nightmares? Does the world even deserve Gen X (that question could be interpreted different ways)?

It's important to periodically ask ourselves what we want out of life. Do we still care about wealth, popularity, or prestige? Are we hell bent to that CEO position? I've noticed that a lot of my Gen X colleagues indeed own (or hope to own) that c-suite, but plenty are professionally content with less. The challenges that come with those offices simply aren't worth it for some. When I find myself unhappy at work, I'm more of a "gas tank half full" kind of guy, meaning it's probably time to drive away and find something new. Life is too short, and the road trip of life must continue. Next step, here I come!

Sometimes I feel like I'm getting too old for such dramatic career transitions, then I remind myself that age is a bullshit way to gauge a life. A better way to measure the worth of your life is to ask yourself how it brings value to the table? Show your work. Your effort. Your results. You can see this ethic in Gen X parenting, which is something that should be studied and utilized for future human development. If you currently have a ten-year-old and you're pushing fifty—guess what? The challenging part of parenting is just beginning. It is so much harder to parent teenagers than adolescents, and it involves more than sitting on the couch for a chat on occasional afternoons. Gen X understands the importance of physically showing up for teens as well as mentally and emotionally. Yes, we want our kids to do chores and learn responsibility like our parents taught us, but we also have to show up with enough energy to engage meaningfully, because this changes how they feel about themselves. The kids deserve this bond, and so do we. That's why it's so important to take care of ourselves too, not just our kids.

Wearing the Gen X badge of honor comes with a price. We don't drift quietly into our graves… we march. No excuses. The no-man's-land of lethargic existence is not in our rulebook. Own it. Build it. Create it. Offer it. Guide it. Respect it. Yet we are often still ignored, underestimated, and discounted. People think of us as the silent generation between Boomers and Millennials because we don't whine and complain about everything. So, it often seems unjust when younger generations mischaracterize our tendency to make do with less as wasted potential… our insistence on minding our own business as the self-absorbed avoidance of responsibility. Fuck that. Gen X still owns the possession arrow. There's still plenty of time left on the shot clock. The Gen X army is a sleeping bear. Maybe it's time to wake the fuck up. There is still time to ride a wave. Take the lead! Create! Innovate! Become who you were meant to be.

For additional inspiration, contemplate some of the gadgets that meandered through the Gen X upbringing. The Walkman, for example, was a noble concept as one of the first mobile electronic gadgets ever offered. The name said it all. Get up, go outside, and walk. Explore the world.

We live in a world where phones and pads suck the energy straight out of our brains. The younger generations have never even experienced an alternative to this lifestyle and now devour isolation in place of interaction. Gen X knows better and should lead by example, even though we are also addicted to gadgets. Younger generations need the support of a non-virtual community with real emotions instead of emojis. They shouldn't have to wait for horrific tragedies to experience the feeling of a community coming together, because humans need that kind of support during the mundane times of life as well.

Video game controllers used to have a joystick and one single button. That's it. Electronic options were few and simple. Yes, the games were basic, but they also weren't nearly as addictive. Sometimes I feel that life needs to loop back around to simplicity. Small changes could go a long way. Long live the analog. Take the long way home. Hold the door for several people, not just one. Focus on others for an entire day and ask people how they are doing (maybe even follow up with second question). Leave the conversation better than you found it.

The cavalry of other generations might be galloping past us, but I have a feeling they aren't stopping to check in at the Gen X corral.

We've been present the whole time, right LL??… Just don't call it a comeback… Gen X never left.

CALL TO ACTION

Lead with generosity, not Wi-Fi speed; real connection still runs on kindness. Leave a place, a space, or a person better than you found them. Invest your attention, energy, and care, in the small moments—they're the ones that matter most.

21

MEAT AND A ROLL

"Wealth consists not in having great possessions, but in having few wants."

—Epictetus

I never really experienced a wide variety of food growing up. Might have been the family budget. Or maybe my mom just wasn't up to pursuing a drawn out, culinary adventure every day while juggling a full-time job. I know that while raising three boys and a husband, her choices had to be limited, on budget, and produced in mass quantities. Hence, I rarely tried anything new. Basic was best. A bowl of sugar-laced cereal for breakfast, a hot dog for lunch, and a frozen pizza for dinner. No joke, this summed up most of my childhood meals. Fruits and vegetables were more like a rumor, than a reality. "Meat and a roll" became my moniker. At restaurants, the servers laughed. At family parties, "Just give Murph some meat and a roll." In hindsight, my plates showed glaring evidence of malnutrition. Awful. I would kill my kids if they tried to pull that with me. As an adult, I try to keep my plates more colorful and healthy.

On a deeper level, I liked the negative moniker. It made me feel important, but for all the wrong reasons. Sure, I remember people telling me, "They are laughing at you, not with you." But life was a joke to me then, even when I was the punchline. I see things differently now, and I take life more seriously. It took me a while to recognize the truth behind the laughter and attention from "friends." They never cared about me or my health and were the last to ever come around to help in times of need. Do you know who your real friends are? Try calling them when you need help and you'll find out (insert cricket chirping sound). The Stoics remind us that the measure of our character isn't what we achieve alone, but how we improve the spaces and lives we touch along the way.

So, no more Meat and a Roll. Take care of your body so it can take care of you. Try new things. Taste the sauce. Put vegetables and fruit on your plate and step out of your comfort zone daily. It's not enough to go to the gym. A healthy person takes care of the mind, as much as the body, so don't settle for complacency. Strip down the walls and barriers. Work on becoming a better version of you. Make the effort to definitively choose which values will define your life and then stand up fiercely for what you believe. Don't worry, confidence will follow and will end up drawing the people who mirror your value into your life, which will bring out the best in you. Fill your mind with reading, music, art, and nourishment, rather than reels and candy. Impress people with your thoughtfulness, your effort, and the arts of preparation, presence, meaningful communication. Just care.

It's way too easy to complain about everything that is wrong with the world. A true measure of control is learning how to make it better by improving the moments and people around you—without seeking validation.

CALL TO ACTION

Do not live on the rations of habit. Step beyond the simple plate. Feed your body, feed your mind, and feed your soul with intention every single day.

22

HARD LABOR

PAPER ROUTE, PENNY SAVER PARTIES, AND PIZZA DELIVERIES

"When you wake up in the morning, tell yourself: The people I deal with today will be meddling, ungrateful, arrogant, dishonest, jealous and surly. They are like this because they cannot tell good from evil."

—Marcus Aurelius

As I write this, I'm looking at a stack of bills and collection notices.

Looking at those envelopes piled on the table brings back memories of my childhood job delivering newspapers. I had to knock on doors with a notebook and a pencil to collect payment from reluctant adults. Back then, the stakes felt enormous when someone didn't pay. I always imagined this sort of worry would go away in adulthood. Turns out, they just get bigger, wear nicer clothes, and arrive in thicker envelopes.

If collection notices aren't motivation for change, then I don't know what is. It makes you wonder: is this what adulthood is about? The constant pressure to earn more, do more, grind harder? Another side hustle, another job, another hamster wheel that somehow never seems big enough? How did I even get here? Reviewing the early stages of my so-called "transient resume," my earliest specialty was in delivery services. I'm talking about day-to-day, door-to-door delivery work requiring repetitive personal interactions. These jobs taught me more about humanity than most college courses ever could. It was part atrocious, part hilarious, part hopeful, and part doomed. You know, like life.

It all started with a paper route. On my Diamondback BMX bike, I used a bungee cord to strap a stolen milk crate onto the front handlebars for the papers. There were about twenty houses in my neighborhood, so the newspaper dailies easily fit into the crate. Every morning before school, I stopped at each house, jumped off my bike, and half-ass folded the papers so they fit into mailboxes. Sometimes, customers insisted that I leave the papers by the front door, but they tipped well, so I didn't mind. When they didn't… well, I'll get to that later. Sundays were different, because the paper was three times the larger due to cartoon pages, inserts, and coupons. It was a fucking monster. On those days, I had to "borrow" a shopping cart from the supermarket to lug all those papers around. The filled cart was heavy as hell to push which meant the route took me twice as long as usual. To make it worse, people got super pissed if the Sunday paper was not there by like 8:00 am. On a fucking Sunday. The nerve!! Walking the streets alone at dawn, I always ran into the same sorts of people: the ones who hadn't slept yet from partying the night before, the ones who didn't have a home, and the ones out looking for trouble. To avoid trouble, I became unusually street-smart at a very young age.

When it came time to collect money for deliveries, I was forced to learn organizational skills. Each week, usually on a Friday, I forced myself to hand-deliver each paper by ringing the doorbell. With a small notepad and pencil (always a #2), I kept a tally of the papers delivered and how much each house owed. Usually it was the same number, but when people went out of town, or just refused to answer the doorbell, their weekly tally increased. Occasionally, a customer did answer the door but didn't have any money.

They only answered the door to tell me to piss off face to face. Fuckers. I was a shy kid, and too intimidated to argue. The worst customers by far were the assholes who didn't include a tip for my services. Please understand, I didn't get paid by the newspaper. In fact, I had to pay the newspaper racket every Saturday for the papers, and they didn't give a fuck if a customer forgot to pay me. I worked only for the tips, so not tipping the paper boy back then was seriously messed up. Most people were pretty good about it, though. Some even gave me a whole dollar, which was a lot of scratch back then.

At the time, I thought non-tippers were jerks. Some of them were. Years later, I realized that life is usually more complex than that. People carry invisible battles you never see from the sidewalk. Bad days. Bad jobs. Bad lives. Marcus Aurelius wrote that people act badly because they cannot tell good from evil. Back then I just pedaled angrily away. Today I try to remember that most people are simply struggling to get through their own routes.

My best days as a paper boy were when I got to deliver the paper to an old man who had a subscription to Playboy magazine! He was married, and his wife was always peering out of their front window and calling my parents my friends and I were up to no good. Playboy magazine back in the 70s and 80s was one of the few nudie magazines around with a traditional centerfold in full photographic effect! Each month, on Playboy delivery day, I brought two papers up to their door instead of one. I left one paper by the door, grabbed the magazine, and hid it inside the second paper as I rushed back to my bike. No idea if the old lady knew what I was up to, perhaps not. Or maybe she was just glad I was keeping the magazines away from her husband. Perks of being a paperboy.

My next delivery job was the Penny Saver route. This route was insane. Each Saturday afternoon, I went to the distribution center to load up five or six enormous stacks of papers. All of the papers were coupons, and all were different. There was no possible way I could have collated this monstrosity on my own, so I dragged my family into service. Each week, we all sat on the floor in a semicircle around the television and stuffed plastic bags while watching Archie Bunker or WWE wrestling. On those nights, we even ate our dinner (hot dogs, of course) right there on the floor while filling the bags. Each bag had circular holes on top used to hang the bag of coupons on people's front doors. The hanging part for me lasted about one week, and then I was just chucking them from the street and praying it landed close to the door. I didn't have to collect any cash or interact with customers on this route (which was 10x the size of my paper route), so I didn't really care if I pissed people off. During this job, I learned that there was an advantage to being a lefty. One was that it made the arc of throwing a Penny Saver from the street to a house land somewhat close to the front door. Usually. Occasionally the plastic bag would rip, or someone (my little brother) wouldn't stuff the bag correctly, and all the contents would fly out all over someone's lawn. Depending on my mood, I would either pick it all up to re-stuff, or (more likely) say "tough shit," and pedal away pretending I didn't notice.

My final delivery job was for a small, but respectable, boutique pizzeria on the border of Berkeley and Oakland. By this time, I was in my mid-twenties and completely lost in the sauce of what I wanted out of life. A couple of Armenian brothers ran the pizzeria, and the entire kitchen staff was Mexican. The brothers were okay mostly, and the cooks had my back, other than always nagging me to go play soccer with them on Sunday mornings. Every Sunday night, they confronted me about not showing up, and every time I told them I liked to sleep in after staying out late on Saturdays. Anyway, when I wasn't in my car delivering craft pizzas with the trusty Thomas Guide (still no cell phones), I stood in the back of the restaurant and folded pizza boxes while listening to the Mexicans talk shit about the customers, the owners, and probably me.

It was a pretty good job, but delivery to any place in Oakland or Berkeley at night was nuts and potentially hazardous. I've delivered to the ghettos and was almost knifed once. I've delivered to a house full of real-life witches (Berkeley). I've delivered to a stoner who always ordered the same shit and always spent an hour searching for money. I've delivered to some flirtatious, bored housewives (at least, I think they were flirting) and to my friends' apartments, who would be seated around a six-foot bong watching reruns of X Files. I delivered to a black activist (Oakland) who always lectured the "cracker" (me, I guess) on how society was and should be… right before handing me exact change, no tip. To be completely honest, if I didn't live in a small, rural town and have an unreliable car, I would think about delivering again, even if just for the stories and personal interactions.

Those delivery jobs were never about the money. Not really. They were front-row-seats to humanity. Wealthy houses, broken houses, kind people, strange people, generous people, angry people. Every doorbell was a small lesson about the world and how unpredictable it could be. When you spend enough time knocking on doors, you eventually realize something important: everyone is carrying something heavy, even if it isn't visible from the outside.

As a homeowner and veteran of the deliverable employment industry, I would like to encourage you to always tip your drivers. Talk to them. Make them laugh. Treat them like people. You may be the best part of their night. Or you could end up as a paragraph in the book they are planning to write.

CALL TO ACTION

Life delivers lessons the same way our newspapers are delivered: one doorstep at a time. Pay attention when they arrive.

23

THE SPIT PIT

"More is lost by indecision than wrong decision."

—Marcus Tullius Cicero

The Catholic school I attended on Long Island had little to no grass or athletic fields. Instead, students used the church parking lot for athletic purposes and assigned the parking stripes as bases or first-down hashtags. It's just the way it was, so no one ever complained. Besides getting hurt if you fell during touch football games (or fighting with other students), the parking lot was our playground. We were also allowed to play in a little alley between the school and the church. The walls were all brick and smooth, and one side of the alley had a set of stairs that went down into a utility room… and the infamous Spit Pit.

The only game we could really play in such a small place was handball. We usually played with about five to ten students, mostly boys, all hustling around in that tiny space slapping balls to the walls as hard as we could. The games were loosely organized, a lot of fun, and a great way to unleash some of the angst we all felt. Occasionally, someone smacked the ball too high, and it sailed onto the roof. This usually ended in expletives and a fight. Now and then, someone tried to climb the rain gutter, but not often because those detentions sucked. The other thing that sucked was when the ball ricocheted over the stair rail and into the Spit Pit.

Before the ball even cleared the rail, chaos reigned and all parking lot activity screeched to a halt. Shouts of "SPIT PIT" filled the air, and it didn't matter if you a handball player or not, EVERYONE came to watch. That's because the person who hit the ball now had to run down the stairs to get it. Simple, right? Wrong. As the unfortunate kid descended, all the other players got to line up around the staircase above him (or her) and spit. Yes, spit. It was disgusting. Some kids couldn't really spit properly, so the saliva sort of daintily stretched down to the person below. Others hocked gigantic "loogies" and aimed with air force precision. It wasn't pretty at all, but when it wasn't me on the stairs, it was so fucking hilarious.

Looking back now, it's kind of amazing what kids can accept as normal. No teachers, no adult supervision, just a pack of feral Catholic school kids inventing medieval punishment systems in a church alley. At the time, stuff like this seemed like just another Tuesday. But if I'm being honest, there were days when I laughed a little too hard while someone else was on those stairs. Kids learn empathy slowly, and sometimes the lesson doesn't get through until years later.

The people on the stairs reacted differently each time. Some retrieved the ball as fast as possible and only got a little spit on them. Some unfortunate souls either tripped or slipped on the way down and were annihilated while assessing for injuries. Occasionally, the person who walked down the stairs was older or bigger, and the spitters were forced to decide if spitting was worth the risk of possible retribution. On most of these occasions, there would be a fistfight as soon as he reappeared from the depths of the pit… also very entertaining. The absolute worst move a person could make during a Spit Pit descension was hesitation. Hesitation ruined kids, because it gave half the school time to get into the perfect position to soak an entire uniform. If you are wondering why anyone ever bothered going down to get the ball, it's because not retrieving the ball you lost earned you the label of coward.

I vividly remember my turns in the Spit Pit. Suck city. I tried to act calm, but speed was the key. "Murph" definitely took the brunt of multiple deluges of various forms of slobber and loogies, but at least I didn't hesitate. In that moment, dignity had nothing to do with staying clean. It had everything to do with showing up and getting the job done.

As barbaric as it sounds, the pit served a purpose—I guess. It sharpened people's aim and improved their handball game. It also taught us that sometimes hesitation in life is necessary, but most of the time it is not. In fact, it can even be a curse. Maturity and confidence come with understanding when it's time to just stop thinking and jump. It's good to use caution sometimes, but at other times we really need to just make the move, take the hit, and get the job done.

CALL TO ACTION

Find the Spit Pit you're hesitating to face. Is it something you fear? An awkward situation you've been avoiding? A question you can't get the nerve to ask? Now, stop thinking, take a deep breath, and start marching. Get that fucking thing done!

24

MUCH LOVE AND FOREWARNING

"Circumstances don't make the man; they only reveal him to himself."

—Epictetus

As a proud Gen X representative, I try to lead by example. It would be easy to sit back and criticize the generations behind us, but that's not the assignment. Our assignment is to show up for others and set the tone. How we communicate with others can become our greatest strength or our biggest challenge, especially when we are frustrated. For those feeling particularly challenged by the world, this section is for you.

I preach the above as though I've always handled frustration well, but that would be a lie. There've been plenty of days when I walked into a room already irritated and convinced everyone else was the problem. It took me longer than I'll admit to realize that bad attitudes don't fix problems—they only spread the misery around.

If you can relate to this and want to see macro level changes in your daily life, try zeroing in on a predictable, daily routine. Life always seems clearer and more manageable when you can focus on things you are able control like small disciplines, repeatable actions, clearly defined expectations, and steady progress towards a goal.

On a micro level, avoid complaining without offering solutions. Just stop. No one respects pure negativity. It's both irritating and unprofessional. If you see a problem, bring ideas. Bring effort. Bring character. But never bring a complaint without a solution.

When dealing with differing opinions, try to voice your ideas to others with confidence, but also with the understanding that your way may not be the best way. I always stress this to coworkers before we enter a conference room to discuss an issue. Please leave your ego at the door and understand that the best answer or solution to a problem may not be yours… and that's okay. You may not like it, but as mature adults, we should all learn to be comfortable with this reality.

Marcus Aurelius penned a great rule of thumb for life, *"Be tolerant with others and strict with yourself."* No matter what people around you are doing, show up every day and get shit done. Even if it's only a small step forward, consistency compounds. "Murph the Greek" finds it very hard to bet against someone that can consistently do this, and it may surprise you to see how quickly your progress can build whether mentally, physically, spiritually, or emotionally.

Ultimately, life is what you make it. The late great Andrew Wood, lead singer of Mother Love Bone, stated that oh so eloquently in his music, but he also lived by the mantra. He treated every show like it was a sold-out stadium, regardless of the shithole dive club he was in. Every freaking show! Go check out the videos. You won't regret it. This sort of enthusiasm is the essence of making the most of life. It's infectious and inspirational.

Other good advice I recently unearthed was to shift focus away from the year of birth and the year of death, and towards the hyphen that sits between the two. What do you want to accomplish in the "space between?" (right, Dave Matthews?). Another healthy thing to remember is that life can be tough and full of bullshit, so it's okay to use the word NO. Say no to what drains you. No to what doesn't fit your capacity. No to what isn't within your path of values. The power of "no" to something that doesn't fit your narrative can act as a shield around your mental health. Use it wisely.

Living in the Deep South with a strong outside-the-box mentality has been difficult. I've definitely learned this the hard way. When you challenge long-standing traditions in a small, southern community, people don't always greet you with open arms. Sometimes those arms are crossed with a glare that says, "Who the hell does this guy think he is?" Those moments force you to decide whether you're here to fit in quietly or to push for something better.

Although traditions can be important tools of bonding and remembrance, I've learned to recognize the dangers within communities whose majority blindly follow traditions simply because "that's how it's always been done." As we grow and evolve as humans, some things must evolve with us to keep us whole, functioning, and protected. Use your head to read the room and consider embracing change when it benefits others.

Whatever you do, never stop learning. The ability to learn something new every day (especially after you turn 40) is an absolute blessing. Don't feel embarrassed of your age or your starting point. Everyone had to start somewhere. A Stoic would remind us that a life without learning is a life asleep. Out of love for ourselves, and for those around us, we are warned not to become stagnant or let habit turn our days into meaningless repetition. Each sunrise offers a new lesson and each challenge a chance to sharpen our minds and widen our hearts. To stop learning is to stop living, so meet each day with humble curiosity and gratitude for a chance to become a bit wiser.

CALL TO ACTION

Move toward what strengthens you. One disciplined step beats a thousand wishes.

25

THE INDEX FUND OF LIFE

*"Waste no more time arguing about what a good man should be.
Be one."*

—Marcus Aurelius

I started thinking about life like an investment portfolio one afternoon while staring at my retirement account and realizing two things: first, I should have paid way more attention to compound interest in my twenties, and second, most of the real wealth in my life had nothing to do with money anyway.

Welcome to the Gen X Fund of Life.

A revolutionary, low-maintenance, anti-establishment vehicle created by those born between 'We landed on the moon" and "Smells Like Teen Spirit." The fund is currently going public and undergoing diversification, so all generations are now allowed to join in on the fun! Forget crypto. Forget hedge funds. Ignore your cousin's wellness startup (since it's probably a pyramid scheme). It's time to put your mind, body, and spirit into an asset class that fully understands the potential weight of existential dread and what it actually means when someone says, "I miss MTV when it played music."

More specifically, A GENXistential Growth Fund is a type of fund that tracks the performance of a specific generational index for all others to profit from by holding a backpack full of insecurities, pop culture references, and latent parental disappointment. Unlike traditional funds that chase trends and waste time with vision boards, Gen X funds sit quietly in the back, eyerolling at your hustle-culture memes, while sipping a flat diet soda.

Fund Name: GENXistential Growth Fund

Ticker Symbol: MEH

Fund Type: Emotionally Passive, Spiritually Diversified, Irony-Weighted ETF

Inception Date: Sometime Between the Fall of the Berlin Wall and the Rise of Grunge

Fund Manager: A Collective of Disillusioned, Yet Hopeful, Gen Xers

Custodian: Your Inner Child (Now with a Mortgage)

Meet our Team!

- **The Portfolio Manager:** The guy wearing flannel with a tattoo he regrets but won't admit it. Tends to grumble at a representative sample of anthems, disappointments, and societal shifts.
- **Strategy Analyst:** The friend who constantly reminds us that maybe quitting our jobs to open a record store was not a sound long-term strategy.
- **Risk Manager:** Our aging knees, lower backs, and doctors who now recommend stretching before engaging in anything remotely athletic.
- **Traders:** A rotating cart of Gen Xers quietly still adapting to adjusting life positions—changing careers, raising kids, caring for aging parents, and pretending they know how TikTok works.

Share our Philosophy!

The GenXistential Growth Fund seeks to match the performance, intensity, and deep-seated sarcasm of its corresponding generational index. Active management is discouraged. Righteous passivity is the key strategy.

Example Indexes:

- The S&P 1965-1980: Tracks midlife crisis memes, pop culture nostalgia, and credible threats to quit all social media.
- Wilshire 867-5309 Total Market Index: A top ten grunge ethos sentiment index weighted by plaid content and anti-establishment lyrics.

Investment Objective

The Fund seeks to achieve long-term growth of mind, body, and spirit by investing in a diversified portfolio of nostalgic memories, sardonic wit, and the occasional hot sauna/cold plunge class. The fund aims to provide returns that align with the Gen X ethos: heavy skepticism with a dash of hope.

Principal Strategies

- Mind Allocation: Invested in critical thinking, sarcasm, and the ability to recall obscure 80s trivia.
- Body Allocation: Focused on "sustainable" practices like occasional jogging, balanced diets (pizza with salad), and ergonomic office chairs.

- Spirit Allocation: Diversified in meditation apps, vinyl record collections, and regular posts connecting deep meaning to a post-modern world.

Risk Factors

- Cynicism Overload: High levels of sarcasm may lead to missed opportunities for genuine connection.
- Nostalgia Volatility: Overindulgence in memories may cause disillusionment in the present.
- Technological Disruption: Rapid changes in technology may outpace the fund's ability to keep up, leading to feelings of obsolescence.

Fees and Expenses

- Management Fee: 0.00% (Because no one wants to pay for someone else to tell us what we already know).
- Emotional Expense Ratio: Varies based on life events, existential crises, and the latest season of your favorite show being cancelled.

Performance Overview

The Wilshire 8675309 Total Market Index: a comprehensive exposure measure of everything we cared about, from rotary phones to rollerblades, and that one summer when everything seemed all right.

Benefits (Still loading… please wait. LOL)

- Stability: Fund durability increased over time due to constant exposure to scorn from Boomers, pity from Millennials, and blank stares from Gen Z.
- Lower Expectation Ratios: Minimal overhead, since no one expects anything from us, anyway.
- Long Term Investment: Low turnover rates because leaving now would mean starting over, and we just can't.
- Tax-Deferred Cynicism: Gains in irony and apathy accrue quietly, taxed only upon overt displays of optimism.

Seeking Investors

Ideal investors in this fund are those actively searching for capital preservation for a swiftly dwindling spirit, high liquidity needs marked by a strong desire to drown sorrows in alcoholic beverages, and an urge to set aside emergency funds in case of deep, overwhelming questioning of purpose. The GENXistential Growth Fund can offer investors measurable wisdom, more functional habitual options, and an alternative currency for managing the daily market volatility of life.

Join Our Team and Expect Results!

Sarcasm aside, the real reason this "fund" exists is because most of us eventually realize that life doesn't reward constant trading. The biggest returns often come from patience—showing up for people, sticking with hard things, and making time when it actually matters. Marcus Aurelius had it right: stop arguing about what a good person should be, and just start acting like one. That might be the most reliable investment strategy ever invented.

CALL TO ACTION

If love is the only currency that truly compounds, spend it daily–kind words, patience, time, and truth will always yield the highest return.

26

THE MIDDLE CHILD OF GENERA-TION X

1971!

"Happiness and freedom begin with a clear understanding of one principle: Some things are within our control, and some things are not."

—Epictetus

I often wonder what it really means to be born in the middle of a generation. Not quite the first, not the last, and always a little overlooked. That's my story: Brooklyn 1971. From the moment I arrived, it was clear that life wasn't going to hand out participation trophies. If anything, it handed out harsh lessons with a side of chaos.

The middle children of the X generation are the folks who were born in 1971. Okay fine, they were born *close* to the middle of the most profound generation that human-kind may ever witness. That's where my story began: Brooklyn, 1971. *Wowzah.* At that time, the United States may have been the land of the free, but there were very few freebies on the streets. Crime was rising, streets were burning, people were surviving. Even the Boomers raise an eyebrow while discussing the hardships of life back then. God's sense of humor must have been at an all-time high when he dropped Generation X into the timeline. We lived a hard-as-fuck lifestyle full of constant mental fires we were expected to extinguish with a broken hydrant. The situation left a mark called The Middle-Child Syndrome, which was defined by the five characteristics below:

1. We're literally sandwiched by dominant person-alities; thus, we tend to adapt quietly to change, adversity, and discomfort. This taught me to observe first, speak later, and develop a radar for bullshit at a young age.

2. Our stories aren't loud, because no one gives a shit about them anyway. But the quiet moments often revealed a lot about our skills and character—like learning how to negotiate, improvise, and survive without applause.

3. Hollywood loves a trope. So do we (I guess that explains the "syndrome"). And yet, the real world rarely scripts things neatly. Middle kids think in the messy in-betweens.

4. We're peacekeepers–but we do it anonymously. Our kind frowns on those who seek the spotlight or drama. Little did the world know, some of us were quietly orchestrating the action behind the scenes.

In other words, we're badass. I should also mention that we have a high sense of independence, feelings of alienation, competitive tendencies, the habit of risk taking, strong social skills, consistent sharing behaviors, and a tremendous capacity for true friendship. In the singing voice of Sophie B Hawkins, I'll just say, "Damn."

The Pulse of 1971:

- The voting age dropped to 18.
- The first email was sent.
- Charles Manson was convicted.
- *All in the Family* debuted. Hilarious… surreal… the comedy of its time. Watch this show if you ever want a glimpse into how the adults in our lives behaved. It explains a lot.

- NASDAQ was founded—and the rich got richer.
- Evel Knievel jumped motorcycles like a madman. Amazing to watch live on TV. CORE action sports are the only thing that comes close to EK's death-defying tricks… except maybe surfing (man vs. mother nature–epic!).
- Led Zeppelin debuted *Stairway to Heaven*. This was Live in Belfast!
- Frazier took down Ali. The fight of the century.
- NPR began. This station has withstood the test of time and is still standing, despite the recent loss of federal funding.
- Amtrack began services, although they also had their first wreck with mass casualties later the same year.
- A previously unknown and crooked legged entry from Central America named Canonero II won the Kentucky Derby, creating the biggest upset in the history of the race.
- Walt Disney World opened its gates. An expensive mousetrap, in my opinion.
- Southwest Airlines took to the skies. Although more recently, they dropped free bags (damn you, Southwest!).

- More coups in more places = more military deployments. People were on edge, and not everyone was buying the government's explanations (sound familiar?).
- Space exploration ramped up with trips to the moon and initiated to Mars.
- May 1st, 1971, marked the day I took the stage.

In 1971, these events set the rhythm for the Middle Ages of Generation X, shaping us into people that learned the weight of choices early and understood the brevity of time. If the proverbial timeline says we only have twenty or thirty years left to make an impression, then I say—fuck it! I'm aiming to be 100! I've decided to keep writing my ever-evolving lists of life (you're reading one now!). I will keep reviewing, editing, and riding the wave of life.

Don't try to fight mother nature, just roll with it. Focus on each issue as it comes. Am I still jamming during the first set? Acoustic for the second? What about the encores? It never ends. But, through all the small, daily decisions you make, this stage of life is the perfect time to focus on your own happiness and freedom for a change. We must ban together and refuse to be intimidated or paralyzed by the noninstinctive nature of current society. Trust in the adaptive skills from our youth to guide us as we roll with the punches.

As we continue to bask within our beautiful, tormented Gen X souls, try to remember how it all started. Look back and really try to regenerate the feeling of your first inspirational moment about the future. For me, it was in that desolate airport terminal replaying the scene with Eddie Vedder… only this time, he turns around to look in my eyes and mumbles, "Murph, just breathe, brother!" So, when the world spins out, I just breathe—and act where it matters.

CALL TO ACTION

You're not done yet–live loud, level up, and keep editing your damn story. Never underestimate the power within the chapters you write today. They are the legacy of tomorrow. Onward…

EPILOGUE

On October 25th, 1993, the Grunge music movement was hitting second gear and not slowing down. When my friends and I heard the rumor that Grunge was set to grace the cover of an upcoming issue of TIME magazine, we knew it was a huge deal. Life back then offered a few simple daily pleasures like the mail truck. The anticipation of that rickety hunk-of-junk barreling down our road was a huge adrenalin rush. As the occupant of the good ol' USPS Glory snapped the mailbox shut and cleared the area, I ran over to pull the family copy of *TIME Magazine* from the stack of bills. I froze… the shot was perfect. Standing center stage, mid yowl, was the lead singer of Pearl Jam. I grew up seeing Reagan, Gorbachev, Nobel Peace Prize winners, and all sorts of other dignitaries and political figures gracing that cover, but this was different. Special. It marked the moment I understood that my generation, Gen X, would be different than the ones before us… and that we were about to take on the world.

The differences we are creating back then are still works in progress, but the overall influence Gen X has had on the world has already been substantial. It's not surprising how much we differ from the generations who followed us, as we represent the final generation of humans to grow up without cell phones or the internet. At times, it feels like we are a different species entirely from younger generations, but I find hope in the possibility that our common humanity will serve to unite, rather than divide, us. What I've learned by writing this book and reexamining my own (often embarrassing) experiences is that Gen X is still very much here and relevant. We are still just winging it, one mixtape, one mistake, one miracle at a time, but we still have a good chunk of life left to live.

Gen X never really waited for permission to engage in life. We just picked up whatever tools we could find and built something out of the scraps of others. That innovation still lives in the very cores of us. The world will continue to change, and that's perfectly fine! Don't be afraid of it. Instead, tap into that old adaptive nature and question it. Create something from it. And refuse to sit still long enough to be defined by anyone else's rules.

That's my final call to action. You don't need a map or a kid to give you instructions. Just trust your instincts like you used to, and remember that mistakes are just a natural part of life. Bring your scars, your stories, and your punchlines to the table of life, and above all remember we are all just making it up as we go. Remember who you are and where you came from, and that's where the rest of your legendary story will begin.

ABOUT THE AUTHOR

Brian Murphy is a Mississippi-based writer blending Gen X sarcasm, stoic wisdom, and a lifetime of questionable decisions. Raised on loud music and low expectations, he now dispenses perspective like a slightly overqualified bartender – equal parts humor, truth, and "how did I get here?" energy.